SETTING THE SCENE

THE GREAT
HOLLYWOOD
ART DIRECTORS

SETTING THE SCENE

THE GREAT HOLLYWOOD ART DIRECTORS

by Robert S. Sennett

HARRY N. ABRAMS, INC., PUBLISHERS

Project Manager: Mark Greenberg
Editor: Ellen Rosefsky
Designers: Dana Sloan and Kingsley Parker
Rights and Permissions: Barbara Lyons and John K. Crowley

Library of Congress Cataloging-in-Publication Data
Sennett, Robert S., 1955–
    Setting the scene: the great Hollywood art directors / by Robert S. Sennett.
    p.   cm.
    Includes bibliographical references and index.
    ISBN 0–8109–3846–4
    1. Motion pictures—United States—Art direction—History. 2. Motion picture
art directors—United States—Biography.
    I. Title.
    PN1995.9.A74S46   1994
    791.43'0233'092273—dc20   94–4556

Printed and bound in Japan

PAGES 2-3:

*The Thief of Bagdad This unusual setting, made to appear underwater in the completed film,
haphazardly confuses Erté-style Art Deco with Aubrey Beardsley's Art Nouveau. (United Artists)*

CONTENTS

COLORPLATES

ACKNOWLEDGMENTS

Writing *Setting the Scene,* like making a movie, required the help of a lot of people. For their advice, assistance, and cooperation, I would like to thank Samuel Gill and Robert Cushman at the Margaret Herrick Library, Academy of Motion Picture Arts and Sciences, Beverly Hills; Ned Comstock and Leith Adams at the Cinema and Television Library, University of Southern California, Los Angeles; Ron and Howard Mandelbaum, Photofest, New York; Brigitte Kueppers, Theater Arts Library, University of Southern California, Los Angeles; and Mary Corliss at the Film Stills Archive, Museum of Modern Art, New York.

Special thanks are also due to my editor, Mark Greenberg, and my agent, Ruth Nathan, who answered all my questions with patience and promptness. In addition, I would like to thank Patricia Rogers and other members of the staff of the Fine Arts Library, Harvard University, for understanding the problems of an author who happened to be an employee. My friend John Malafronte had to live with this book since he lives with its author, and for putting up with me he deserves my unstinting admiration.

Setting the Scene is dedicated to my father, Ted Sennett. Dad: Your expert advice and faith sustain me. You are my inspiration, and I love you. This one's for you.

INTRODUCTION

When Cecil B. DeMille completed work on *The Ten Commandments* in 1923, he decided it would be easier to bury the entire set in the sand than to drag it in pieces back to Los Angeles, one hundred miles to the south. Conceived by the famed French Art Deco designer Paul Iribe, this City of the Pharaohs had gates 120 feet high and nearly 800 feet wide. The black statues of Ramses II were 35 feet high. Twenty-one sphinxes lined the city's main avenue.

The sets for *The Ten Commandments* are among the most magnificent ever built for a Hollywood movie. Yet for sixty years this modern-day archaeological treasure trove was ignored, if not forgotten. When an oil company decided to drill in the Guadalupe Dunes in 1983, the site's precious secret was revealed. Two filmmakers, Bruce Cardazo and Peter Brosnan, have been trying to raise money to dig up part of the set and restore it in the Smithsonian Institution (as well as to make a film about their discovery). Digging may already be under way, but the sand is winning; by 2090 the shifting dunes will have obliterated any trace of Iribe's work.

Yet, half-destroyed and buried, the sets for *The Ten Commandments* are still in better shape than any other Hollywood film set of equal age, all of which have long since been destroyed. Nothing remains of the work of the great Hollywood art directors except the fragile nitrate stock on which the films were printed and a few blueprints and plans. Even recent art direction such as Norman Reynolds's work on *Raiders of the Lost Ark* (1981) or James D. Bissell's work on *E.T.: The Extraterrestrial* (1982) would have been lost if not for a second life as a featured attraction in a theme park.

This book is an attempt to reclaim the accomplishments of the great art directors before the sands of time obliterate our memories as surely as the actual sand of the desert will wipe out DeMille's Egypt.

The "art director" of the twenties, should he have called himself one, would not recognize the "production designer" of the nineties. The first film sets were built to resemble the stage so as not to confuse the actors and the audience, who were accustomed to the conventions of the theater. Film space asserted itself very quickly, however, and soon an entire range of special effects—from forced perspective to miniatures—were available and accepted. Advances in design and in technology went hand in hand, as new lighting techniques, faster film, sound, and eventually color each in turn forced the art director to reevaluate his style and expand the vocabulary of film design. By the seventies, computer operators had begun to replace painters and carpenters, and today film design is a technical craft as complex as scientific engineering.

What an art director or production designer actually has done depends on the era in which he was working and the studio (or production company) for which he worked. At MGM, Cedric Gibbons's contract required that he receive credit for all the studio's films whether he designed them or not. His powerful personality and demand for centralized control put his visual stamp on MGM's product for thirty years—sleek, elegant, and tasteful to the end, almost regardless of the subject of the film. On the other hand, a modern designer like Dean Tavoularis, who works most frequently with Francis Ford Coppola, bends his tastes to the particular film, producing immediate, individual, and intense work like *The Godfather* (1972) and *Apocalypse Now* (1979).

Any attempt to generalize the working habits and personality traits of the great art directors and production designers is likely to fail. They were frequently talented and prolific draftsmen. Some, like Anton Grot at Warner Brothers and Jack Martin Smith at MGM, began their careers as sketch artists but quickly adapted to the role of executive as their power and influence increased. Others, like Boris Leven at Columbia or William Cameron Menzies, liked sketching and continued to draw in several different mediums until they retired. Autocratic types with a strong visual sense (like RKO's Van Nest Polglase) were evenly matched by more chameleonlike figures such as William A. Horning at MGM or Hal Pereira at Paramount, who could work in any genre and for any director with equal ease.

In the end, and despite the tremendous changes in technique and custom, the film experience today is not so different than it was many years ago. A great movie must still tell a story, contain likable heroes and heroines and convincingly evil villains, and be interesting to look at. The tools may have changed, but the product is still the same. *Setting the Scene* is both a tribute to the golden age of Hollywood art direction and a booster's guide to contemporary masters. By bringing together the best of all ages, from the earliest silent masterpieces to the most recent blockbusters, this book hopes to show the kinship of quality and emotional satisfaction that links them.

SILENT SPACES: ART DIRECTION BEFORE SOUND

The first art director was a carpenter.

Frank ("Huck") Wortman had been D. W. Griffith's chief carpenter since *The Birth of a Nation* (1915). Griffith's ability to discern talent probably helped him pick out Wortman from the hundreds of technicians working on his films and slowly elevate him to a position equal in honor and responsibility to his chief cameramen, Billy Bitzer and Karl Brown. Yet Huck Wortman's fame is entirely retrospective; during his career he received not a single on-screen credit.

In the wide-open world of filmmaking before sound, before the calcification of the studio system, art direction, like every other aspect of filmmaking, was uncharted territory. The first films utilized the painted flats and boxlike sets of the stage, and little was done to create the illusion of reality. Audience dissatisfaction with filmed plays influenced silent features, which slowly began to display the kind of settings and special effects that would, by the mid-twenties, be known as "art direction."

Never in the history of cinema has the relationship between the fine and the lively arts been so close as during the golden age of silent films, roughly from 1914 to 1925. Several

The Thief of Bagdad (1924) *Douglas Fairbanks as the thief helps show off Anton Grot's use of white and gray shapes to define film space and William Cameron Menzies's sense of scale. (United Artists)*

factors are responsible for this. The studios had money, and artists always needed money. The tragedy of World War I had left Europe morally as well as physically shaken. Old values, the values that had led the world to war, were being questioned by young and old. There was a celebration of the experimental and the new, and this celebration took place most conspicuously in the arts, in the books of writers like James Joyce, in the paintings of artists like Pablo Picasso, and in the music of composers like Igor Stravinsky.

The cinema fit the bill: it was new and modern. Many of the men who would go on to become great Hollywood art directors were born in Europe and grew up in this period of intellectual foment and artistic freedom; the greatest contributions to the history of art direction in the cinema would come directly from Europe.

ABOVE: *A Trip to the Moon (1902)*

Drawing ("Right in the Eye!"). The earliest film sets were no different from those of the theater: two-dimensional painted backgrounds. (Méliès)

BELOW:
Filmmaking in Wellsburg, West Virginia, c. 1917. Sometimes even the cast and crew could be forgiven for thinking they were on the stage.

A set from an unidentified silent production,
c. 1917. Eventually, the public's demand for
increased realism in the pictures encouraged film-
makers to build large, elaborate sets.

ABOVE: *Intolerance* (1916)

Source material for the Babylon sequence: French fin-de-siècle painter Georges Antoine Rochegrosse's "The Fall of Babylon." D. W. Griffith and other silent-era directors often relied on Victorian sources for their historical dramas. The results, though far from accurate, were impressive. (Griffith/United Artists)

RIGHT: *Birth of a Nation* (1915)

Set still of Ford's Theater. The first master of cinematic space was D. W. Griffith. For many years the size and scope of the sets in his films were the standard for art direction in Hollywood. (Griffith)

The Ten Commandments (1923)

The oxcarts being built. In many cases the materials and techniques of art department employees were as preindustrial as the settings the employees were hired to depict. (Paramount)

The Cabinet of Dr. Caligari (1919)

The birth of film design as character. Francis (Friedrich Feher) and Alan (Hans von Twardowski) greet Jan (Lil Dagover) on a seriously disturbed street corner. (Decla-Bioscop-Goldwyn)

THE CABINET OF DR. CALIGARI

In the years following World War I, Berlin was a center of artistic activity in Europe. The movement labeled "Expressionism" began there. In painting, Expressionism took the form of violent color and clashing shapes; in literature, strongly felt emotions. Very soon the movement attracted international attention, and it was inevitable that its artistic conventions would be attempted in the new medium of film. The first and still most successful attempt was *The Cabinet of Dr. Caligari* (1919).

Caligari is primarily the work of four men: the director Robert Wiene and the designers Hermann Warm, Walter Röhrig, and Walter Reimann. All four worked in Berlin, and they all knew Herwarth Walden, the leading agitator for the Expressionist movement in Germany and editor of the influential magazine *Der Sturm.* From Walden and his circle, Wiene and his designers learned the basics of Expressionist art: the portrayal of space as filtered through the emotional state of the subject, and the use of abstraction and geometry to render the portrayal in two dimensions. These qualities, in a nutshell, are what make *The Cabinet of Dr. Caligari* so important to the history of film design.

The film begins innocently enough in what appears to be a pleasant garden. A sad-looking young man watches an equally sad-looking, and somewhat inexpressive, young woman walk by. The man, challenged to memory by the sight, begins to relate a tale to his companion in the garden. Suddenly, we are in the town of Holstenwall. The "town," such as it is, is clearly a painting on the wall in the back of the set. The fairground includes painted "tents" and a merry-go-round whirling at a terrifyingly wrong angle. We have entered the world of *Caligari.*

The remainder of the movie—a gruesome tale of the mad doctor and Cesare, his murderous, sleepwalking charge—unfolds within this illogical space. Every detail of every set is subjugated to the rigor of Expressionist distortion: chairs with no right angles have seats perched five feet off the ground, and the houses have trapezoidal windows. Most memorable are the streets of Holstenwall, three-dimensional abstract compositions of receding angles, jutting parapets, and brightly lit blank spaces. Francis, the young man who began narrating the story, watches as first a town clerk, then his friend Alan—and very nearly the woman he loves—are killed by the somnambulist Cesare under Caligari's control. Only at the end of the movie—in a concluding "frame" imposed on the filmmakers by the studio—do we realize that Alan is an inmate in an asylum, and Caligari is his beneficent overseer.

The effect of *The Cabinet of Dr. Caligari* on the film world in Europe and the United States was immediate and profound. American critics, though slightly confused, were mightily impressed. In a 1921 article in the *Mentor,* Hugo Ballin, a notable painter and designer who went to Hollywood in 1915, described the sets as "futurist" and called the backgrounds "scenery that acts." An anonymous writer in *Current Opinion* called the settings "post-impressionistic" and credited the cameraman with creating the settings, but still managed to note that the film "marks an epoch in the movies."

Caligari opened in New York in April 1921. So far as can be determined, though the film caused quite a stir and instituted a "code" of set design for monster movies for a decade or so, only one contemporary attempt was made in America to imitate the film's peculiar charm. Dorothy Davenport, Wallace Reid's widow, made *Human Wreckage* (1923), a story of drug addiction, and used a proportionally distorted street scene to represent the twisted viewpoint of the addict. The screenplay, in fact, specifically called for something "like Dr. Caligari's cabinet" to express the drug-warped world view of the movie's protagonist. It was not a hit.

SET DESIGN IN EUROPE

The influence of *The Cabinet of Dr. Caligari* was felt more directly in Europe than in America and in a more subtle way. Rather than consciously imitate the distortions of Warm, Röhrig, and Reimann, many film designers working in Europe after the war borrowed only the spirit of their work and strove to create settings that integrated the characters with the world they were supposed to live in, thereby enhancing the meaning of the film. Many of these masters, when they immigrated to America, brought this conception of art direction to Hollywood and used it to create the foundation of modern film design as practiced by the big studios throughout the thirties and forties.

Among the notable European film designers was

The Cabinet of Dr. Caligari

Cesare (Conrad Veidt) with Jane (Lil Dagover) on the ramparts of the city. (Decla-Bioscop-Goldwyn)

The Cabinet of Dr. Caligari   *The somnambulist Cesare (Conrad Veidt) murders Alan (Hans von Twardowski) in a frenzy of angles. (Decla-Bioscop-Goldwyn)*

Metropolis (1926)

Model of Babel. Metropolis *provided the earliest and one of the most successful examples of the "Schuff-tan" process—the combining of miniature models with full-scale sets and actors. (UFA)*

Lazar Meerson, who worked his entire brief life on the Continent (he died in 1938 at the age of thirty-eight). Meerson designed two spectacular sets for director René Clair, the street scene for *Sous les Toits de Paris* (1930) and the factory for *A Nous la Liberté* (1931). Also notable is Hans Poelzig, an architect who designed strikingly modern buildings and interiors for *The Golem* (1920). Several continental art directors who achieved fame and success in America—among them Anton Grot, Hans Dreier, and Alfred Junge—designed films in the most up-to-date style in their homelands before emigrating.

Perhaps the most famous and influential art direction in a silent film coming out of Europe after *Caligari* was found in Fritz Lang's *Metropolis* (1926), designed by Otto Hunte, Karl Vollbrecht, and Erich Kettelhut. Sketches by Hunte and Kettelhut preserved in the Cinémathèque Française show them both to be extraordinarily proficient draftsmen in the Art Deco style. The gleaming metallic towers and machinery and the geometry of the interiors in *Metropolis* are testaments to the

designers' ability to translate their drawings into the convincing illusion of three dimensions. Furthermore, as a purely visual primer, *Metropolis* set the standard for science-fiction imagery for forty years to come.

The most interesting aspect of *Metropolis* from the point of view of the art direction, however, is not the sets themselves but how they got to the screen. Eugen Schufftan was a cinematographer working on the film; he devised a way to save the studio money by combining models with full-size actors and partly built sets. In an era when special effects such as dissolves, iris shots, and fade-outs were created in the camera, Schufftan pointed the way toward a future of three-dimensional manipulation, laying the foundation for the entire Hollywood special-effects industry.

Despite Huck Wortman's good work, by the beginning of the twenties a number of factors had brought an end to the era of carpenters-as-art-directors in Hollywood. One of these factors, previously mentioned, was the audience's increased demand for—and expectation of—more realistic and spectacular effects. Another was the rise of Hollywood itself. The artists' colony and health resort that was Los Angeles in the teens was rapidly becoming a thing of the past, as one by one the big studios moved their technical operations from New York to the endless sunshine of southern California. Along the way, independent producers, of whom D. W. Griffith was the prototype, disappeared into the conglomeration of the studios. Likewise, naive types like Wortman were replaced by sophisticated designers—like Wilfred Buckland and Cedric Gibbons—who had cut their teeth in New York, were educated in the arts, and most importantly, knew how to speak producer-ese, an increasingly baroque and oblique language.

It is a myth that Hollywood in its silent days was "innocent," or that the films made there were "quaint." The studios, though not as rich and powerful as they would be in the decades to come, were still far and away the most glamorous place for a person to work—and work they would. By the end of World War I, the United States had surpassed England, Germany, and France in the number of new productions, and by the mid-twenties lots were lit nearly around the clock. The star system was fully in place, and the clamor for pictures starring Theda Bara, Gloria Swanson, Mae Marsh, Francis X. Bushman, Wallace Reid, and Douglas Fairbanks, to name just a few, was as great as it would be for their counterparts twenty years later.

Furthermore, silent film was not technologically inferior to later sound film. It has only come to seem that way due to years of neglect as well as miscomprehension. Fragile nitrate stock easily disintegrates. Projecting the film at the wrong speed, disregarding the musical scores and cues that accompanied almost every major release, and ignoring the hand-tinted copies that were frequently distributed to theaters in major cities all distort the modern perception of what these films looked like.

Luckily, no amount of trickery has yet obscured the incredible visual accomplishments of the first generation of Hollywood art directors. Their awesome and at times unsurpassed accomplishments—all without computers, panchromatic film, and sometimes even electricity—remain one of the most accessible of pleasures when watching silent film, either in a theater or even on videotape, because the visual design is so clear that it is instantly intelligible.

DOUGLAS FAIRBANKS

In the early days of the Hollywood star system, no star was bigger than Douglas Fairbanks. Two films Fairbanks made for United Artists (the company he founded) in the mid-twenties, *Robin Hood* (1922) and *The Thief of Bagdad* (1924), are America's first masterpieces of art direction. Although they were the work of different design teams, they have the same look because of the unifying effect of Fairbanks's personality. He had the determination to realize his dreams and the money and the power to do so. In an era when production and turnover were the building blocks of the business, Fairbanks stood out by emphasizing quality.

The art direction in *Robin Hood* was principally the work of Wilfred Buckland, who began his career in New York, designing settings for the theatrical producer David Belasco. Belasco was famous for introducing realistic effects on the stage at a time when Victorian artifice was still popular, and Buckland did much to contribute to his success. Buckland went to California to work with Cecil B. DeMille, but his style of gigantism combined with lyrical, dramatic lighting was best suited for Fairbanks. The castle Buckland built for Robin Hood and his merry men to plunder was, at 90 feet, the tallest structure ever built for a picture to date. Buckland had access to a library of material documenting the clothing, architecture, and settings of the Middle Ages that Fairbanks had assembled just for this production—the prototype of the modern research department.

Fairbanks himself was afraid he would be unable to compete with the decor. After getting his first look at Buckland's enormous sets, he reportedly told the director, Allan Dwan, "I can't compete with that!" Dwan had to sweet-talk him into it.

THE THIEF OF BAGDAD

Robin Hood was Douglas Fairbanks's signature historical epic, and *The Thief of Bagdad* was his signature fantasy. All the elements that made *Robin Hood* so tantalizing come together in *The Thief of Bagdad* to make it still, after seventy years, one of the most totally satisfying entertainments Hollywood has ever devised. And, of course, the art direction is a good part of the reason.

The person charged with creating the scenes and special effects for *The Thief of Bagdad* was William Cameron Menzies, one of the great names in the history of Hollywood art direction. Menzies was born in Connecticut and studied art and architecture at Yale and at the Art Students League in New York. According to his coworkers, he got his break in the business at a delicatessen on West Fifty-sixth Street called Hendricks, just around the corner from the Art Students League. There Menzies met Anton Grot, who was at the time designing films for director George Fitzmaurice. Grot quickly understood Menzies's genius, took him to be his protégé, and ended up collaborating with him on *The Thief of Bagdad.*

Who did what on the production is not clear: the film credits read "art director, William Cameron Menzies; associate artist, Anton Grot." Grot had the greater experience with perspective drawings and understood the principle of camera distortion. He made charcoal drawings of the sets in the correct perspective for filming. It is likely that Grot designed the sets on paper and Menzies worked day to day on decorating them, developing the drawings into models and supervising the special effects. Both Menzies and Grot turn up again later: the former for *Things to Come* (1936), which he directed, and *Gone with the Wind* (1939), the latter as the art director of choice for Warner Brothers in its gangster and swashbuckler days.

The mood of *The Thief of Bagdad* is completely evoked by the setting of the very first sequence. Against a background of clouds and stars, a swamilike figure begins to tell his story . . . and we are on the main street of Bagdad, where flocks of people go about their business flanked by immensely tall, smooth walls. We sense that these walls were built to be insurmountable, but within moments Fairbanks appears, swings up and over every obstacle, and disappears into a hole in the ground. Thus, through the use of the sets, Menzies has established that we are in a world of fantasy and that the character played by Fairbanks is different from the others: he is a thief, and the constraints—both moral and physical—that restrain the others do not apply to him.

From here on, Menzies and Grot continually play with juxtapositions of character and scale to underscore and increase our perception of the fantasy elements of the story and to emphasize how the thief is different

from ordinary people. At one point, Fairbanks hides inside an enormous clay pot; at another, he is hanging from an elaborate Moorish balcony, stealing lunch. At times, the art direction goes for out-and-out spectacle, such as the parade of princes trying for the hand of the princess with whom the thief has fallen hopelessly in love. In this scene, director Raoul Walsh and cameraman Arthur Edeson have deepened the focal point of the lens to reveal hordes of armies traveling from the horizon, each identified by intricately detailed national costumes (designed by Mitchell Leisen, later to be a minor art director and major director himself). At other times, the director and the art director have collaborated to give an intimate moment an extra fillip, such as the early scene where the thief is being flogged. Here the thief is shown in a midrange close-up, revealing primarily Fairbanks's Christ-like face (a reminder that Jesus was crucified between two thieves?). Behind him there are a few dark steps leading to nowhere and a portion of a blank white wall. This shot alternates with a deeply focused establishing shot of the spikes to which the thief is lashed and the huge town square full of people and buildings, reinforcing the thief's sense of isolation.

It is possible that the first half of *The Thief of Bagdad,* based so strongly on Moorish fantasy architecture, is primarily Grot's, and that the second half, with its

OPPOSITE, ABOVE: *Robin Hood* (1922)

A gatefold production still of the castle being built. Wilfred Buckland's castle was the biggest single set built in Hollywood to date. (United Artists)

RIGHT: *Robin Hood*

The castle completed. Note the small orchestra in the foreground entertaining the cast and crew. (United Artists)

The Thief of Bagdad

This unusual setting, made to appear underwater in the completed film, haphazardly confuses Erté-style Art Deco with Aubrey Beardsley's Art Nouveau. (United Artists)

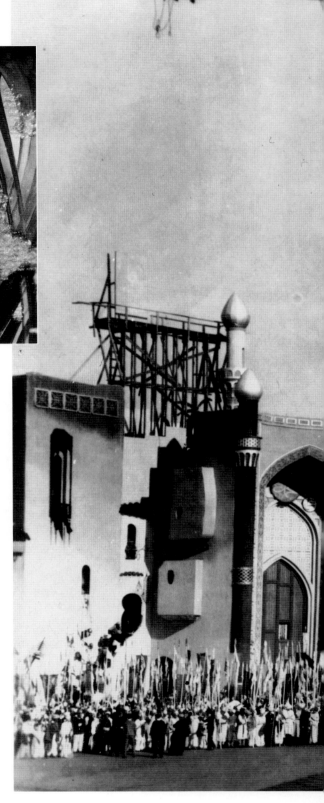

The Thief of Bagdad

This set sketch, probably made by an assistant working for Anton Grot, shows how amazingly close the construction of the completed city came to the artist's original conception. (United Artists)

The Thief of Bagdad Douglas Fairbanks's film (designed by William Cameron Menzies and Anton Grot) is one of the greatest glories of Hollywood art direction. The neon sign announcing Bagdad high above the city gates does not appear in the film. (United Artists)

Sous les toits de Paris (1930)

At the end of the silent era, the integration of the built set and
realistic detail was complete. The golden age of art direction
was about to begin. (Cinémathèque Française)

set pieces and special effects, is the work of Menzies. Whatever the division of labor, the film—from a design point of view—explodes with inventiveness once Fairbanks leaves the city to begin his quest for the ultimate present to win the hand of the princess. Menzies creates one effect after another, each more magical than the one before it. First comes the City on the Hill, and the first use of miniatures in the film. This is followed in close succession by the Hermit of the Defile (a small, hairy man and very large papier-mâché boulders), the Valley of Fire (where cameraman Edeson was called upon to do some tricky double exposures relating to leaping flames), the Valley of the Monsters (including a smoke-blowing lizard), the Old Man of the Midnight Sea (underwater special effects), the Abode of the Winged Horse (an Art Deco–style planetarium), a Cloak of Invisibility (self-explanatory), and, as a grand finale, the famous flying carpet, probably the most spectacular effect yet attempted in the cinema's young history, a combination of miniature and process shots, hydraulics, and actual wire-guided flying. If this description seems literal and rather long, see the movie. It is the birth of film design as star.

Panchromatic film arrived in 1924. Partial sound was a reality by 1926. By the end of 1929 hardly any silent films were being made. The silent era, even the era of black-and-white, was coming to an end. The effect of these changes on the industry was profound. With pictures costing more and more money to make and production and attendance down due to the Depression, the producers established a stranglehold over their productions. The unit system instituted by Irving Thalberg at MGM in the early thirties turned the production of feature films into a factorylike procedure, with teams of technicians (director, cameraman, set decorator, costume designer, etc.) working on assigned productions and reporting to a central producer, who then reported to Thalberg. This could not help but make all but the most complacent film designer chafe under the collar—and make the independent-minded and unaffiliated employee extinct.

From 1928 the studios reigned king. There was the old guard: MGM (Louis B. Mayer), Paramount (Jesse Lasky), and Fox; the up-and-coming: Warner Brothers, Columbia (Harry Cohn), and Universal (Carl Laemmle); and the small conglomerates: RKO, Samuel Goldwyn, and David O. Selznick. Independent production was dead. The amount of money it took to mount a production that could compete in quality with the studios was prohibitive, and distributing the finished film in a world where the studios controlled every theater was impossible. Thus very few pictures were not affiliated in one way or another with one of the studios.

Although there were disadvantages to the studio system, there is a reason why so many of the pictures produced by the studios are masterpieces. From the mid-twenties until the disintegration of the studio system in the late fifties, the studios had the money and the talent to do whatever they wanted and an audience that shared their beliefs and expectations. It was a narrow but complete universe, vastly different from the endless and fragmented one the film industry lives in today. Studio art directors, scenic designers, and set decorators were instrumental in creating the explosion of images that accompanied the rise of the sound feature as it spread across America and the world. The sound era was born.

CITY STREETS, SMALL LIVES: HOLLYWOOD'S AMERICA

When Edward G. Robinson and Douglas Fairbanks, Jr., got out of a car to rob a lonely suburban filling station at the beginning of *Little Caesar* (1931), this event symbolized the arrival of a new era in motion picture—and American—history. *Little Caesar* was the first notable sound gangster film. But the greater significance of this first scene is in its underlying assumptions: America was a nation full of displaced and disgruntled citizens desperately pursuing idealized dreams of wealth and fame.

In 1900, 60 percent of the population of the United States lived in rural surroundings; by 1930 this percentage had shrunk to barely 40 (and by 1960 it would be less than 30). Americans were moving to the city, and the problems of city living—overcrowding, poverty, and crime—were there to greet them. As always, Hollywood perceived an opportunity to comment upon and exploit the situation.

By 1930 Hollywood too was changing. The Depression brought plunging profits. The cost of switching to sound killed off many of the smaller, independent studios and caused the larger ones to cut costs, merge, and trim stars and staff. A few individuals grew more powerful, both in the front office and on the set, and the first glimpses of what became known as the "house style" appeared. MGM had glitz and stars (and supervi-

Little Caesar (1931) *As Otero (George E. Stone) and Rico (Edward G. Robinson) rise in the criminal world, their surroundings*

sory art director Cedric Gibbons). Paramount evinced continental sophistication through its chief art director, Hans Dreier. There were gritty realism and low budgets at Warner Brothers with art director Anton Grot, and up-to-date elegance at RKO, with Fred Astaire and sets designed by Van Nest Polglase.

In the years between the advent of sound and the end of World War II, it was particularly Warner Brothers and Paramount that did the most to portray the inner workings of this new urban America, its world of speak-easies and nightclubs, of grifters and molls, and of ordinary Americans caught without jobs or hope, seeking something to alleviate the endless frustration of their lives.

LITTLE CAESAR

Warner Brothers was the first studio to sense the yearning of the public for urban fables and the first to address that yearning in *Little Caesar.* This film successfully

portrays the lives of Jazz Age gangsters, setting up the paradox that would characterize the genre: be your own man, be loyal to your friends and family, be ambitious, but don't challenge authority, don't break the rules, and never be greedy. This mixed message is at the heart of all crime movies; it is what gives them their strangely sympathetic stars and dramatic tension.

Little Caesar tells the compact, cautionary tale of Cesare Enrico Bandello (Edward G. Robinson) and his rise and fall as the leader of the gangs of the North Side of Chicago in the twenties. Bandello, known as "Rico," begins his career in crime with the stickup of the gas station and the probable murder of its night attendant, and moves up relentlessly until there is nowhere else to go but to his death. His constant admonitions to his favorite, Joe Massara (Douglas Fairbanks, Jr.), to "have your own way, be someone," and his lust for big touring cars and fancy "joints" are perversions of everyman's American dream. His demise is foreshadowed by a title card before the story begins that reads, "He who lives by

Little Caesar

Joe Massara (Douglas Fairbanks, Jr.) and Cesare Enrico Bandello, known as "Rico" (Edward G. Robinson), stop for spaghetti after robbing a gas station. (Warner Brothers)

the sword shall perish by the sword." The audience realizes from the start that true independence and freedom are hopeless desires and that hard work brings small rewards—but the only alternative is death. This is a somber and bitter pill, swallowed as entertainment.

The sets for *Little Caesar* were designed by Anton Grot, the veteran art director of nearly two dozen films for George Fitzmaurice, Douglas Fairbanks, Sr., and Cecil B. DeMille by the time he arrived at the Warner/ First National lot in 1927 at the age of forty-three. Grot was already established as one of the finest draftsmen in the business and one of the great designers of spectacles, having worked with William Cameron Menzies on Fairbanks's *The Thief of Bagdad* (1924). For Mervyn LeRoy, the young director of *Little Caesar,* Grot used his talent for chiaroscuro to create shadowy images of urban night life; crass, nouveau riche palaces; and poverty-ridden ruin to suggest Rico's rise from and return to the gutter.

Grot's sets sometimes set off Rico's physical smallness against the overwhelming massiveness of the society he is trying to conquer (Robinson himself was a small man). In one scene early in the film, when Rico is leaving the office of the soon-to-be-deposed boss Sam Vetori, Robinson is squeezed by the vortex of a huge, descending staircase and the railing of the balcony—he's a tiny, black-hatted dot pinned like an insect against the wall. Later, after Rico is ostensibly the king of the North Side, Grot's set reinforces the futility of Rico's climb. Rico is sitting in his office (the same office Sam once had, now redecorated to suit his glitzy taste), lounging on a couch in a gaudy smoking jacket. But the set hints of Rico's fate even here: Robinson is again trapped between the strong, dark verticals of the sloped loft ceiling and the crushing perspective of its slanting walls.

Throughout *Little Caesar*, Grot's designs serve to remind us of the class differences between "successful" and "unsuccessful" gangsters, and of how transient the differences between them can be. Sam's office at the Palermo Club is furnished like any successful middle-class businessman's, with a big desk and chair, the only notable difference being a conspicuous bottle of liquor. Top gangster Arnie Lorch's office is much glitzier, with the Spanish-style architecture that was very much in style at the time, potted palms, a library, and a carved oak desk and mantelpiece. Eventually, Rico (and Grot)

Paramount's supervisory art director Hans Dreier in his library, showing off a miniature.

Double Indemnity (1944)

Walter Neff (Fred MacMurray) in the lobby of his office building. Ordinary, even drab, and uncompromisingly realistic settings were the hallmark of film noir. (Paramount)

work their way up to "big boy"–type decor, with 50-foot ceilings, an immense glass chandelier, and rococo details in the picture frames, andirons, and chairs. Yet Rico ends up dead in the most plebeian of sets, a street. Moments before his death, Robinson is framed by this set, again a small black figure dwarfed by the blackness of the night. He passes behind a billboard advertising Joe Massara's revue, titled "Tipsy Topsy Turvy." That pretty much sums up Rico's predicament and the circle of settings that *Little Caesar* uses to frame his rise and fall.

FILM NOIR AND NOSTALGIA

The city in a Hollywood picture is often a place of death. *Little Caesar* may have popularized this concept, but motion pictures had been associating urban environments with tragic endings at least as far back as *Sunrise* (1927), and they continue to do so today. Beyond death and decay, the image of the city in Hollywood films also has been traditionally one of nostalgia, a looking back at a time of innocence and inexperience from a position of jaded sophistication. This can be done ironically, as in *Little Caesar,* and more recently it has been a form of camp re-creation, as in *Batman* (1989), with its 1980s take on a superstreamlined, totally cinematic urban America that existed only in the movies, never in real life.

The core of this nostalgia, its most sophisticated and poignant use in strictly visual terms, is the genre produced by Hollywood that has come to be identified by the term "film noir." Of these films, the most exemplary are two by Billy Wilder, designed by Hans Dreier, *Double Indemnity* (1944) and *Sunset Boulevard* (1950). Both are told in the form of flashbacks, the purest form of nostalgia, by men who are or who are about to be dead. And both are designed with one eye on the innocent past and the other on the rotten future, with sets that greatly contribute to the story by transplanting the viewer into the past, a past that exists only on the screen. The best film noir thus doubly explodes the myth of cinematic realism, having actual correspondence neither to the world as the viewer knows it nor to the world as it existed in the past, but only to the unreality of Hollywood.

Part of this nostalgic displacement is due to the fact that both *Double Indemnity* and *Sunset Boulevard* are set in worlds far apart from the world of the years in which they were released. *Double Indemnity* is set in 1936, near the end of the Depression, a distant point from the war-wracked and industrious America of 1944. In *Sunset Boulevard* the gap is even wider: the gulf between Joe Gillis's postwar job hustling and Norma Desmond's presound memories of Hollywood in the twenties. It is this separation of time and place and their expression in the sets that make these films so evocative and so perfectly paired.

DOUBLE INDEMNITY

By 1944 Hans Dreier had been the head of Paramount's art department for twenty-one years. He was largely responsible for the elegant look of the studio's films, especially during its heyday in the early thirties. He designed several of Josef von Sternberg's films with Marlene Dietrich, including *Dishonored* (1931) and *The Scarlet Empress* (1934), and created the decadent playlands of Ernst Lubitsch's *Trouble in Paradise* and *One Hour with You* (both 1932). It was against these expectations that Dreier designed the most purely American film of his career, *Double Indemnity.*

By the standards of the day, *Double Indemnity* was a film that should not have been allowed to be made. The story, written by James M. Cain in 1936, has extramarital sex, murder for profit, and countless other related illegal activities. Although Barbara Stanwyck was

more than willing to take on the role of Phyllis Dietrichson as a way to break loose of her typecasting as a comedic heroine, no one wanted the more sympathetic but still amoral role of Walter Neff. Eventually, Billy Wilder's legendary persistence convinced Fred MacMurray to play against type, to posterity's benefit.

There are two cities in *Double Indemnity*—Los Angeles, characterized by Neff's Pacific All-Risk Insurance Company and its main hall of identical desks, rows of steel filing cabinets, and black telephones, and Glendale, with the Dietrichson home and its *faux* hacienda–style architecture and nouveau riche decor. These two sets, with a few location settings and Neff's apartment, comprise the sum of Dreier's sets for the film, and this very simplicity itself is part of the effect. What Dreier is helping Wilder say is that one does not need the outward trappings of temptation to go astray, and that anyone, given the necessary circumstances and opportunity, could succumb. This is one of the central tenets of film noir.

Dreier's associate art director on *Double Indemnity* was Hal Pereira. It was perhaps Pereira's instinctual naturalism that tempered Dreier's usual exuberance in creating the simple, understated sets for *Double Indemnity,* which was Pereira's first film. He would go on to replace Dreier as the head of Paramount's art department when Dreier retired in 1950, and he helped create the sets for several of Paramount's late classics, in particular *Shane* and *The War of the Worlds* (both 1953).

The theme of *Double Indemnity* is established with the first shot, again—like the opening of *Little Caesar*—with a car speeding alone at night. In this case the location is downtown Los Angeles and the destination is not escape but surrender, as Neff staggers back to his office to dictate his confession of murder to his boss, Barton Keyes (Edward G. Robinson). As Neff begins his tale, we flash back to his first meeting with Phyllis, and against the dark of the L.A. night Dreier and Pereira evoke a nostalgic suburbia with children playing ball in the street. When Stanwyck makes her first appearance, she is dressed completely in virginal white.

This basic juxtaposition of dark and light, while a cliché, is the dominant visual element of film noir in general, and of Dreier's work in *Double Indemnity* in particular. The two illicit lovers meet at first in the daytime, then only at night. MacMurray is constantly sitting in the dark or turning off the lights—in his office, in his apartment, even, with Stanwyck at the scene of the murder, in his car. In the bright lights of Jerry's Market, Stanwyck wears dark glasses, as if light would reveal the deception in her eyes. They choose a street on the way to the train station to commit the murder primarily because it is dark—all in a city notable for its dazzling sunlight.

Two scenes in particular showcase the use of dark and light on the sets of *Double Indemnity.* The first is that electrifying moment when Keyes comes to visit Neff at his apartment to speak to him about the "little man" who keeps bothering him in regard to the investigation of the murder of Mr. Dietrichson. Unbeknownst to Keyes, Phyllis was already on her way up to the apartment for a liaison with Neff, and she has to hide behind the apartment door to prevent her discovery and the guilt it implies. Disregarding the fact that someone designed the door wrongly (when has a front door to an apartment ever opened out?), the scene plays as a perfect distillation of the setting, as Keyes stands in the hallway bathed in artificial light, while Stanwyck clings for her life to the black shadow thrown by the open door. MacMurray, in the middle literally as well as symbolically, stands halfway between dark and light, framed by a dark door farther down the hall.

The second noteworthy scene is when Neff shoots Phyllis in her home. With "Tangerine" playing poignantly in the background, Phyllis first shoots Neff, who is merely wounded; Phyllis is framed against the shadow of the slatted Venetian blinds. Then Neff shoots her, and he is the one standing in the shadows. On one level, this is pure visual poetry, with tiny alternating bands of dark (evil) and light (good) enigmatically framing each of the protagonists. But on another level, they are just blinds, a perfect example of the way a great art director can allow the simplest of sets to be meaningful. When we come back to the present, to Neff talking into the Dictaphone, the nostalgia is drained of its charm.

The art direction is, of course, not always directly responsible for the effects of darkness and light. A good portion of the credit must go to the director, in this case Wilder, who chooses how to use the set, and to the cinematographer, here John F. Seitz, who helps the director film it. But someone has to think about putting a lamp on a table before it can be turned on, or installing the blinds to filter the light, and that person is the art director,

who, in cooperation with the producer and the director, participates in the development of the movie from its inception. Dreier's and Pereira's art direction for *Double Indemnity* was essential to the success of the film.

SUNSET BOULEVARD

When it comes to expressing the tragedy of nostalgia through the technique of film noir, no movie surpasses *Sunset Boulevard,* a film that is about nostalgia—for Paramount's past, specifically, and generally for our collective innocence before the Depression and World War II. Again the city is Los Angeles. Again the director is Billy Wilder and the art director is Hans Dreier, this time assisted by John Meehan. And again the film opens with a montage of a speeding car, or cars, in this case.

But the police cars crashing into the frame in the opening sequence of *Sunset Boulevard* are not concerned with the expiation of confession but with the certainty of death. There is a flashback, but only to the very recent past: the setting is meticulously the present. The nostalgia in the movie is self-referential: to the movies, not to any reality. For *Sunset Boulevard* is the swan song of old Hollywood, and Dreier's art direction is an homage to old Paramount. It was the last film he would design for the studio he had served for nearly thirty years.

The centerpiece of *Sunset Boulevard*—effectively the only set in the entire film—is Norma Desmond's mansion. The building was indeed a real mansion, though not actually on Sunset Boulevard but on Wilshire, not as tony an address. It was built by an eccentric (but very successful) businessman in 1924, deserted a year later, and left to molder until J. Paul Getty bought it and rented it to Paramount for the film. The owner's principal provision was that the studio build a pool. This pool became the first and last setup in the finished movie, the place where Joe Gillis is, figuratively speaking, laid to rest. (The original opening scene, of Joe in conversation with other corpses in the morgue, was cut after providing hilarity instead of wonderment at an early preview.)

Into this seedy shell of a mansion, Dreier poured the booty of a quarter of a century of prop acquisitions. Every exotic object ever used in the history of Para-

Sunset Boulevard (1950)

Norma Desmond (Gloria Swanson) among her souvenirs. (Paramount)

mount Pictures and still lying around in the property department seems to have been pressed into service: dusty mock tapestries, stained-glass windows, Art Nouveau desk lamps, medieval iron sconces, heavy Victorian picture frames, and chinoiserie—with all attempts at period authenticity or even coordination thrown to the wind. In this film satirizing the vanity of old Hollywood, Dreier is satirizing—and paying a loving tribute to—his employer, Paramount Pictures. Look, the house is saying, this is what is left of your dream palaces; let's say good-bye one last time to this tangled shamble of props.

For Desmond they are props. She has given up the possibility of ever separating her on-screen and off-screen persona, and so has re-created the movie inside her head as her—and our—virtual reality, from the

prow-headed gondola that functions as her bed to the hundreds of gilt-framed publicity photographs that surround her like tiny, glittering mirrors. It is Joe who is the outsider here. He suffers the ultimate penalty, death, for daring to point out that the empress has no clothes.

In every way *Sunset Boulevard* is a finale. It is the last gasp of a great studio whose days as an independent power in the industry are over. It is the farewell appearance of a style of filmmaking that put glamour and illusion ahead of reality. And it is the last glimpse of the old Hollywood, the city within a city where people could walk into Schwab's Drugstore one day and come out a star. (Joe walks into Schwab's a couple of times during the movie and he comes out dead.) Dreier certainly knew this at the time he was working on *Sunset Boule-*

vard; the film is the ultimate tribute to the vanishing world that decades earlier he had helped to create.

THE BEST YEARS OF OUR LIVES

The end of World War II meant a lot of things to different people. To the big Hollywood studios, it meant the resumption of the antitrust suit instigated by the federal government in the thirties that would, by forcing the studios to divest themselves of their theater holdings, rob them of whatever remaining power they still held. Against this background, and that of the ensuing paranoia over Communism and the almost pathological desire to return to the normalcy that first the Depression and then war had destroyed, Hollywood created two late golden-age masterpieces of art direction, *The Best Years of Our Lives* (1946) and *The Big Heat* (1953).

The Best Years of Our Lives tells the stories of three returning veterans and the difficulties they face reentering civilian life. The three veterans are Al Stephenson (Fredric March), a moderately successful banker; Homer Parrish (Harold Russell), a middle-class boy who lost both his arms; and Fred Derry (Dana Andrews), a soda jerk from a broken home. The sets were designed by Perry Ferguson in collaboration with George Jenkins.

Ferguson uses choice details to fill us in on the economic background of each of the principal characters. Al's apartment is in a luxury building—we see the enormous lobby with its twenty-four-hour guard before we see the apartment. Homer's family lives in a modest but pleasant suburban house, with trellises inside and out. Fred is obviously lower class—his father and stepmother live conspicuously next to the railroad yard, the fence has fallen in, and the interior of the house has paper shades and exposed pipes. Each of these settings belongs to the individual character who lives in it; the only extensive interaction between the three veterans is in public spaces, such as Butch's bar or the Café Deauville.

The cinematography on *The Best Years of Our Lives* is by Gregg Toland; Toland and Ferguson had worked together earlier on *Citizen Kane* (1941). Toland's legendary "deep focus," revealing the details of the settings behind the characters, served Ferguson well

LEFT: *The Best Years of Our Lives* (1946)

A set reference still, Bullard's drugstore. (Goldwyn/United Artists)

LEFT, BELOW: *The Best Years of Our Lives*

Art director George Jenkins's charcoal sketch of Homer and Wilma in Homer's garage. (Goldwyn/United Artists)

BELOW: *The Best Years of Our Lives*

A pen-and-ink and charcoal sketch, probably by George Jenkins, of the Stephensons' bedroom. (Goldwyn/United Artists)

ABOVE: *The Best Years of Our Lives*

*A set reference still, interior of airplane.
(Goldwyn/United Artists)*

RIGHT: *The Best Years of Our Lives*

*A set reference still, Butch's bar. (Gold-
wyn/United Artists)*

in *Citizen Kane*. The two of them, working here for
William Wyler instead of Orson Welles, create similar
intricate miracles. Wyler frequently uses mirror shots to
illustrate the difficulties the principal figures have in
understanding the changes that have overtaken their
lives since the war began. There is one in the taxicab in
which Al, Homer, and Fred first arrive in Boone City,
when their anxious faces are reflected in the rearview
mirror, and another when Al checks out his mustache in
the mirror at home, and again when Peggy, Al's daughter,
meets up with Marie, Fred's wife, in the ladies' room of
the Embassy Club.

Literal mirror shots are replaced with figurative
ones, as Wyler reuses sets from earlier in the film in a
more knowing way later on, as in the hallway of the
Stephenson home where Myrna Loy first saw her returning husband in a memorable scene, now the setting for
an argument between father and daughter over her love
for Fred. The most stunning trope of this sort occurs in

the confrontational scene in Butch's, when Fred and Al
argue about Peggy. As the two characters try and fail
(for the moment) to find a common language, the
wooden arches of the bar's ceiling link them silently,
hanging over them and connecting them visually in a
way that their dialogue cannot. This foreshadows their
eventual reconciliation and is a literal illustration of the
film's message: despite our differences, we can perse-
vere. It was a message very much needed in the
years immediately following the war, a Hollywood
happy ending.

THE BIG HEAT

In *The Big Heat* we leave the semiurban world of
Boone City in *The Best Years of Our Lives* for Kenport, an imaginary big city, rife with violence and corruption. Its happy ending, with Glenn Ford's Dave

The Big Heat (1953)

The Kenport police station. (Columbia)

Bannion vindicated and the city's crime boss behind bars, is mitigated by the earlier murder of Bannion's wife and, in the concluding gunfight, the death of Debby (Gloria Grahame), his principal informer. *The Big Heat* is noir without nostalgia, set ruthlessly in the present and without sentimentality; Bannion is almost as inhuman as his adversaries in his desire for revenge.

The Big Heat was one of only two major noir films produced by Columbia (*In a Lonely Place,* 1950, also starring Grahame, was the other). It was directed by the great Fritz Lang, of *Metropolis* (1926) fame, and the art direction was by Robert Peterson, who spent the fifties with the studio and also designed *In a Lonely Place* as well as half a dozen other hard-boiled dramas, including *Knock on Any Door* (1949) and *The Garment Jungle* (1957). Columbia, like Warner Brothers, never had the budgets to mount spectacular stagings, and its art directors tended to cover their sins with lots of day-for-night shooting and recycling of materials.

Peterson's solution for *The Big Heat* was to construct half a dozen realistic interiors, all mildly differentiated by a piece or two of furniture and something hanging on the wall. Lang cut the story at such a breakneck pace that the audience barely has time to notice the setups. The scenes change thirty-one times in less than ninety minutes.

Among the settings is Mike Lagana's mansion, with its miniature gold-framed oils and four-poster bed, all watched over with hypocritical piety by a large portrait of Mama Lagana. The Retreat, one of the nightclubs Lagana controls, is a popular, if low-class, joint, with pin-ups on the walls and the latest in vertical blinds hiding it from the street. In contrast, Bannion's home is the epitome of middle-class taste, with bay windows, mock-colonial features, and even a baby carriage on the lawn, while his "office" at police headquarters is a plain, shabby desk with wanted posters taped to the wall behind it. Over everything there is a fog of cigarette smoke, symbolizing the cloud of deceit that touches every character, guilty or innocent.

Unlike *Double Indemnity,* we never really see the city in which all this corruption is taking place—just a glimpse of some twinkling lights from the balcony of Lagana enforcer Vince Stone's apartment and an exterior shot of a strip of neon-lit nightclubs as Bannion follows Debby out of the Retreat. The presence of the city is codified in the activity of the principals, working either in behalf of those who are paid to run the city or for those who are paid to protect it. As Debby, Grahame sums up Peterson's sets and their role in *The Big Heat* when she walks into Bannion's room in the Marlin Hotel for the first time. "Hey, I like this," she says, looking over the tiny room with its single bed, night table, and plain walls, "early nothing."

With *The Big Heat,* Hollywood effectively closed the door on an era of mock realism. The following year Richard Day's stunning location work for *On the Waterfront* would forever alter the public's level of tolerance for cinematic conceits. It would be a later generation of directors and designers, using splashy color and special effects, who would renew the filmgoing public's romance with urban America on the big screen.

THE COLOR OF THE CITY

In the years following the end of World War II, the motion picture industry fractured and nearly dissolved. The consent decree that forcibly divorced the major studios from their theater distribution chains broke the industry's financial back. Then the rising popularity of television removed Hollywood's previously captive audience. The result: the end of the classic era of the great Hollywood studios.

The producer-driven picture, with its studio-assigned cast and crew, gave way to the "package deal," in which an independent producer or director would put together his own personal creative team and sell the idea to a studio for distribution and publicity purposes only. The concept of a "supervisory art director" like Cedric Gibbons at MGM or Hans Dreier at Paramount was moot, since there was no longer a studio "look" to maintain. Add to this the end of the monopoly of Technicolor (by 1960 most films were being shot on the more muted Eastmancolor stock), a rise in location work, dramatically increased budgets, and specialization by craft, and the result is a clear picture of the state of Hollywood—or what was left of it—by 1970.

The nation that was going to the movies had changed. Fully two-thirds of its citizens now lived in urban surroundings, and the realization that these surroundings were—and always had been—crime-ridden, corrupt, and threatening filled the newspapers and television broadcasts of the day. Sooner or later Hollywood would have to respond.

As the mechanics of filmmaking became costlier and more specialized, the role of the art director changed. Without the massive resources of a studio art department, with its property warehouses and stock sets (now often destroyed after they were used), more than mere supervision was needed. The look of the film had to be carefully visualized in every detail, then created nearly from scratch. The former task was now the realm of the production designer. Although the term "production designer" dates back to the late thirties, when William Cameron Menzies used it to describe himself and his relationship to *Gone with the Wind* (1939; Lyle Wheeler was the art director), the term did not come into general use until the seventies. Now it was truly the production designer who was the star, conceiving the look of a picture and managing the creation of its visual elements. The nominal art director now functioned as the production designer's assistant, the role previously assumed by the studio unit's assistant art director.

Strangely enough, given Hollywood's new permissiveness and its professed adoration of gritty realism, the best productions of the last thirty years—at least from the point of view of the art direction—have been set in mythic spaces, though they concern themselves with the lives and times of city people and American life. Truly realistic dramas such as *Raging Bull* (1979) or *Midnight Cowboy* (1969) have deliberately modest and iconoclastic art direction. The stellar art directors of our day have done their best work in the realm of hyper-reality, a realm that exists only in two dimensions, on the screen.

CHINATOWN

Chinatown (1974) is a landmark film in the history of Hollywood art direction. Along with *The Godfather, Part II* (also 1974), it is the first masterpiece of period design from the poststudio age. Its blend of actual Los Angeles locations with loving but kitschy interiors set the standard for film design for the next dozen years.

Chinatown was designed by Richard Sylbert, one of the preeminent names in the field since 1960. Sylbert

began his career in television, then moved to film in the mid-fifties, studying with William Cameron Menzies. He has been nominated for an Academy Award a half-dozen times (and won twice—once for *Who's Afraid of Virginia Woolf?* in 1966, and a second time for *Dick Tracy* in 1990). In addition, he was the production designer on such notable films as *Reds* (1981) and *Frances* (1982).

The basic story line of *Chinatown,* as stated by John Huston as the patriarch/businessman Noah Cross, is "find the girl." Over the framework of this mystery, director Roman Polanski and screenwriter Robert Towne have laid a subplot involving the water rights to the city of Los Angeles and the underlying corruption of its appointed and elected officials. Sylbert has translated this domain of secrets and mistrust into an unremittingly parched landscape of brown, red, and white. It is Los Angeles, 1937, and there's a drought going on. Every building is sun-baked white, all the men's suits are sand-colored brown, and even the furniture is sepia and red.

Sylbert's task in *Chinatown*—the task of every modern art director re-creating a historical period—is to help the audience travel through time. This is very different from the goals of a historical drama during the golden age of the big studios, when the art director's task was to re-create a space. Audiences unused to the conventions of visual representation, and seeing them for the first time in black-and-white, needed only the illusion of the past to be convinced of its reality on the screen. In the last thirty years or so, the general public's visual education has been greatly enhanced—primarily due to television—and the illusion of space is no longer adequate. We need that elusive dimension of time. This illusion is dependent on a total media assault: the cinematography, costumes, and music are as important as the props and the sets. Indeed, cinematographer John A. Alonzo treated *Chinatown*'s film stock to increase its amber glow. But the props and the sets are the stage, and must be in place for the illusion of time to be complete.

In *Chinatown* small details, the most convincing kind, come to mind. One thinks of Jake Gittes (Jack Nicholson) and his office, with its orange Venetian blinds, big brown leather desk chair, and a bottle of amber-colored booze. Or of the Los Angeles County Hall of Records, with its orange walls, brown carved oak doors, and clouded glass partitions. (Sylbert has said that he deliberately chose clouded glass for this and other scenes to enhance the mystery.) There is even, at one point in the film, a glimpse of a two-dollar bill. Add in the overemphasized costumes (designed by Sylbert's sister-in-law, Althea Sylbert) and the big-band music playing in the background, and the production begins to feel less like 1974 than 1937—except that it is 1937 as remembered in 1974, a transplantation, not a re-creation, of the time. The most successful art directors bring about this transplantation by giving the audience the details it expects to see. A plain (but entirely appropriate) office setting or actual workaday thirties kitchen would strike the modern audience, not familiar with the actual setting, as untrue. Heightening realism with just the right amount of cliché is what makes period re-creations such a difficult challenge.

Chinatown ends with a stagy scene in the heart of its namesake neighborhood, as Jake finds Evelyn Mulwray (Faye Dunaway) trying to run away with her sister and confronted by her father, Noah Cross. As the scene progresses and explodes into accusations and eventually gunfire, the multiple complexities of the plot are dramatically resolved in a rush of sentiment and ambiguity. The visual effect is that of incompleteness: Evelyn is dead, and in the brown-gray smoke of Chinatown and car exhaust and tired detectives, Jake leaves the scene with a very big seventies-style question mark hovering over his head. Irresistibly, there was a sequel to *Chinatown,* produced in 1990, called *The Two Jakes,* directed by Nicholson himself. The production was designed by Jeremy Railton and Richard Sawyer based on Sylbert's designs. It was not a hit.

RADIO DAYS

Another film set in the past that relies overtly on nostalgia for its appeal is Woody Allen's *Radio Days* (1987). Nostalgia is the subject of *Radio Days,* as director Allen takes us on a sentimental tour of the Brooklyn of his youth and the radio personalities that filled his childhood daydreams. Allen's production designer for this film was Santo Loquasto, who has worked primarily in the theater and consequently brings a pleasant staginess to his sets of the family's Brighton Beach household, the

radio studio, and a jet-set nightclub in Manhattan.

Radio Days begins, appropriately enough, with a dark screen and a voice-over, as if it were a radio. When the set is bright enough for us to see anything, the first thing we see is a radio. The tune playing is "Dancing in the Dark." Thus, within a minute, Loquasto has helped Allen visualize the emotional boundaries of the film. All the subsequent design decisions enhance the illusion of a perfectly remembered—and ultimately imaginary—lost world. There is a brief shot of the red-curtained ballroom where the red-vested orchestra members are playing the song that is being broadcast over the radio, an even briefer shot of the family at home, then a little girl singing in front of a gigantic advertisement for bread, as Allen intones, "Now it's all gone, except for the memories . . . "—and this film.

The settings of *Radio Days* alternate between the house in Brighton Beach and the studio and nightclub in Manhattan, with brief side trips to Coney Island and the beach. The signature set of the movie, the one that defines its sense of a loving but lost memory, is the roof of the nightclub in Times Square. This set appears twice—once about twenty minutes into the film as the cigarette girl (Mia Farrow) and a radio personality climb up to the roof for a tryst and get trapped, and again as the last scene of the movie, when, several years later, the nightclub revelers watch the ball drop over Times Square on New Year's Eve.

Actually, it is not truly a set, just a stage with a backdrop, as would be expected from a theatrical designer such as Loquasto, but what a backdrop: a 10-foot-high neon-lined derby, an enormous old-fashioned Pepsi-Cola sign, the Loew's theater marquee, and of course the Camel Man blowing his famous circles of white smoke. This set encapsulates the meaning of *Radio Days*; it presents New York City as a dream world of glittering lights and swank, happy people, of cacophonous noise and dizzying heights, as a young boy—or a middle-aged man recollecting his impressions as a young boy—would remember it. As one of the assembled guests exclaims: "Look at all the lights. What a city this is!" We can't help but agree, even if we never actually saw New York in the forties.

As the snow starts to fall on the crowd—the same Hollywood snow that fell in 1946 on James Stewart in *It's a Wonderful Life*—and another midnight ticks by, Allen reminds us that these "voices grow dimmer and dimmer," and we feel his sadness for the disappearance of a world that, for us, existed only for ninety minutes or so on the screen.

BLUE VELVET

Blue Velvet (1986) is designed with a theatrical conceit like *Radio Days,* but used to a completely opposite effect. Whereas *Chinatown* and *Radio Days* employ sets imbued with the past as a way of bridging the gap between then and now, *Blue Velvet*'s settings are ambiguously contemporary, but so unrealistic that they have the feel of the past and consequently a distancing effect on the viewer's relationship to the characters and action of the film.

The settings for *Blue Velvet* were designed by Patricia Norris; it is her only credit as a production designer to date. Norris is a costume designer, and she has taken the theatrical qualities inherent in the instincts of a costume designer and exploded them to the level of the look of the entire film. *Blue Velvet* begins and ends literally with a curtain—in this case a rippling blue velvet one, enhancing the effect of a nightmare staged for our benefit, and our benefit alone.

With a director as strong and stylized as David Lynch, it is not easy to tell how many of the decisions regarding the settings of the film are original to Norris and how many are her interpretations of Lynch's suggestions. But there are several examples in *Blue Velvet* of the setting as stage, and the audience as voyeur, in which the art director's decisions were crucial.

The first and most extensive use of the set as stage comes during the sequence in which Jeffrey Beaumont (Kyle MacLachlan) and Dorothy Vallens (Isabella Rossellini) are interrupted in their attempt to make love by the psychopathic Frank Booth (Dennis Hopper). The scene takes place in Dorothy's apartment. Jeffrey flees, naked, into her bedroom closet and through the wooden slats of the closet door watches Frank's brutalization and eventual rape of Dorothy. He is horrified by what he sees and yet is forced to watch, as are we. All the elements are reminiscent of a theatrical performance: Frank's ritualistic behavior regarding a glass of bourbon and a strip of blue velvet, Dorothy's forced "sirs," the carefully

arranged chair. The importance of this scene as a visual element in the film is underscored by its length—at over twenty minutes it is one-sixth of the entire film.

The second "stage" Norris designed for the characters of the film to perform upon is the place where Jeffrey and Dorothy are taken after their discovery in Dorothy's apartment, presided over by the drugged and effeminate Ben (Dean Stockwell). There, inside a room that looks partly like the bedroom of a house of prostitution and partly like a cheap nightclub, Ben lip-synchs to Roy Orbison's "In Dreams" with a handheld spotlight doubling as a microphone, while the puzzled and terrified pair, accompanied by Frank's henchmen and a couple of large, bouffant-wigged middle-aged women (the matrons guarding Dorothy's kidnapped son), look on.

Finally, to complete the nightmare's circuitous route from innocence to experience, the film returns to Dorothy's apartment, where Jeffrey discovers a tableau of death: several corpses, including one stuck in a vertical position like a store-window dummy. When Frank returns to confront him, Jeffrey retreats to the closet in which he hid the first time, and the final staging of the confrontation between good and evil is witnessed from private, front-row seats. The next morning, Jeffrey's "good" girlfriend, Sandy (Laura Dern), says to him, "It's a strange world, isn't it?" This is hardly reassuring; a moment later Norris and Lynch drop the final blue velvet curtain, and the movie is over.

THE GODFATHER, PART II

Any discussion of contemporary Hollywood would not be complete without mention of the two cornerstones of the industry for the past twenty years: the sequel and the blockbuster. These two types of film share a cynical regard for the intelligence of their audience and a reliance on formulaic stories, characteristics not inclined to produce memorable work of any lasting quality. Indeed, the current worship of the box office has produced such forgettable films as *Halloween III* (1983) and such self-congratulatory ones as *Romancing the Stone* (1984). But occasionally a sequel can surpass its original, and a film devised to meet the market's needs can be of high quality. *The Godfather, Part II* and *Batman* are prime examples.

The Godfather, Part II (1974) *A staged parade, a real street: art direction in Hollywood, seventies style. (Paramount)*

The Godfather, Part II (1974) is, on the whole, a richer and more complex film visually than *The Godfather* (1972)—a fact later obscured by the release of the two films together as one six-hour videotape. It is also one of the stellar accomplishments of perhaps the greatest art director to emerge in the poststudio age, Dean Tavoularis. Tavoularis first made a splash—albeit a bloody one—working with Arthur Penn on *Bonnie and Clyde* (1967), with its sixties counterculture take on the exploits of a pair of thirties bank robbers. He worked with other directors until meeting up with Francis Ford Coppola in 1972 for *The Godfather,* and the two have been collaborating ever since, most astoundingly on *The Godfather, Part II* and *Apocalypse Now* (1979).

The Godfather, Part II tells the stories of young Vito Corleone (Robert De Niro) in Sicily and New York (a "prequel" to the first film) and the older Michael Corleone (Al Pacino) after Vito's death. The tragic and ironic parallels between the two lives resonate in the film's art direction. The two "halves" of the movie differ in color and design. Similar contrasts occur within segments, creating a kaleidoscope of cinematic tension.

One of the ways in which *The Godfather, Part II* exceeds *The Godfather* in scope and value is the way Tavoularis's choices underscore the moral values (or lack thereof) the characters and the screenplay express. The chief means of achieving this, and the most subtle because it is used in practically every scene, is the symbolic use of color. In a scene at Lake Tahoe, on Michael Corleone's estate, a large blue car is seen. The car is unnaturally blue, which is the point. In the Corleones' world, bright colors are unnatural; only black and blood red are real. The blue car is one of dozens of examples in which the brightness and joy of the outside world, in the form of primary colors, intrude upon the Corleones and make them look all the more morbid. Indeed, at one point the deep browns and blood reds of Michael's den appear to have spread to his face.

An extended simile of this kind occurs later, in one of the most dramatic sequences in the movie. In a flashback to Little Italy in 1917, we see young Vito stalk and murder the old capo Don Fanutti while a traditional Italian feast is celebrated on the street. Fanutti greets his flock dressed in a bright white summer jacket and a white hat. There are hundreds of multicolored strings of lights hanging overhead; there are bursts of firecrackers.

Young Vito climbs up to the rooftops, watching Fanutti pass through the crowd and arrive at home. There Vito breaks in, puts out the light in the hallway, and shoots Fanutti point-blank with a gun wrapped in a bright white towel.

Tavoularis's use of symbolic color provides the audience with small associations that expand the significance of the scene. Fanutti's white jacket and hat are outward signs of purity, but they are also targets. So is Vito's white towel, which, also symbolically, catches fire from the exploding gunpowder and burns red, then turns charcoal black, the color of death. Vito himself is dressed in dark colors.

In terms of light alone, Tavoularis's sets are equally expressive. The brightness of the crowded street contrasts with the lonely showdown in the dark hallway. This metaphor—of public spaces versus private spaces—appears continually throughout *The Godfather, Part II.* Examples include the juxtaposition of the white church interior during Michael's son's First Communion with the dark brown and orange recesses of Michael's office, or the green and blue of a lawn party with the leathery gold and black of the Senate hearing rooms. Immediately after the scene in which Vito kills Fanutti, as if to emphasize the importance of color in signaling the meaning and moral path of the character's lives, Coppola flashes forward to the Corleone's East Coast estate at Christmas. The entire landscape is covered with snow, a double symbol in which the white equals purity but the coldness of the snow equals death. Coppola and Tavoularis would try to do this again, in *The Godfather, Part III* (1990), but unfortunately the visual impact of *The Godfather, Part II* could not be easily duplicated.

BATMAN

Batman (1989) is the apogee of the new Hollywood—self-referential, genre-blind, and production-oriented in ways the old Hollywood never dreamed of. The notorious marketing of this film, with its bat logo appearing on virtually every kind of consumer item in America months before and after its release, merely detracts from its estimable charm, particularly its Academy Award–winning production design by Anton Furst.

Furst created a hybrid universe that is neither a

realistic, contemporary view of a modern city nor a nostalgic view of the past, like that found in *Chinatown* or *Radio Days.* Everything is gray: the buildings are stone, the elevated highways are girders, and a gray mist spews out of smokestacks and manholes everywhere. Even interiors like the newsroom are smoked over. Old-fashioned (and obvious) matte paintings stand in for scenic backgrounds when it seems that models and computer animation would have produced more realistic results. For instance, in one establishing shot, a strangely shaped funnel-topped building is capped by a smokestack emitting clearly stationary smoke. Buildings like Gotham City Hall come whole out of the twenties, while Batman (Michael Keaton) hides in a Neanderthal-era cave watching the entire proceedings on a very up-to-date video monitor. Historical accuracy is not one of Furst's aims—and why should it be? It is neither 1939 nor 1989 but just an ordinary day in Gotham City.

Furst's knowing references to the history of film design are also characteristic of the new Hollywood, capable of revering and lampooning its own past simultaneously, and, more importantly, realizing that the audience will get the joke. At one point, the Joker (Jack Nicholson) sabotages a chemical plant with a lever-turning and knob-pulling fit straight out of Charlie Chaplin's *Modern Times* (1936). Near the end of the film, director Tim Burton shows in quick succession a tiny Batplane circling a model castle tower like the Wicked Witch of the West in *The Wizard of Oz* (1939), then diving into the canyons of the city like Luke Skywalker in *Star Wars* (1977), and then soaring majestically (and in slow motion) across a full-moon sky like Eliot on his bicycle in *E.T.* (1982).

One other key element of *Batman*'s visual style is Burton's use of overhead and low-angle shots of Furst's sets and designs to enhance the sense of vertical space in the movie and to differentiate between good and evil in a symbolic way. We frequently spy upon the Joker from above, for instance in the scene in which he litters the floor of his home with paper dolls. Likewise, we often "look up" to Batman as he drops in through a skylight to thwart the Joker's ransacking of the Flugelhorn Art Museum. Not only are these kinds of shots visually interesting, they are also incidentally a good way to enhance the illusion created by a painted backdrop, rear projection, or a miniature model that, seen from a normal angle or for too long a time, might not appear as convincing.

Batman is a vibrantly beautiful film. It is tragic that we will never know how successful a career Furst might have had; he took his own life in 1991, barely two years after his greatest professional triumph.

Over fifty-seven years separate the black-and-white back alleys of *Little Caesar* from the color-washed boulevards of Gotham City in *Batman,* and yet there is a startling unity to their conception of urban America, one that is precariously balanced between the lure of evil and the struggle to be good. The tools are different—what would Anton Grot be able to do with today's computers, robotics, and supersensitive color stock? But these two films and all the others that share their vision have at their heart the trials of the human spirit. Their sets are our Garden of Eden, and their characters are our Adam and Eve. Some sin and are punished; some resist and triumph. It is Hollywood moral sentiment at its best.

FLESH AND FANTASY: THE HOLLYWOOD MUSICAL

The Hollywood musical was born on Broadway and died on Broadway. Many of the first movie musicals, like *42nd Street* and *Golddiggers of 1933* (both 1933), were set in an actual New York theater and formatted after old vaudeville revues with a little backstage intrigue thrown in for the plot. And the last ones—at least the last produced under the old studio system—were the cinematic versions of proven Broadway hits like *Carousel* (1956) and *West Side Story* (1961). These were basically problems in translation (i.e., how to adapt the Broadway staging to a film format) and not entirely new works of art. The most accomplished musical treatments in Hollywood history, and the greatest achievements in art direction in the genre, belong to the original musicals written for or adapted to the screen and produced by MGM: *The Great Ziegfeld* (1936), *The Wizard of Oz* (1939), and *An American in Paris* (1951).

At the start of the sound era, the genre of the musical in itself posed a new challenge to Hollywood producers, directors, and designers. How would it be possible, with the intimacy and naturalism inherent in film technique, to show characters bursting into song without their looking ridiculous? Should the settings be as realistic as possible, or stylized? These fundamental questions have always plagued

42nd Street (1933)

Busby Berkeley's Times Square—bright, clean, and full of dancers. (Warner Brothers)

filmmakers as they try to discover the perfect combination of dramatic effects, technical wizardry, and pure talent that will create a unified production.

42ND STREET

One early example of a movie musical where the settings played an important part in the integration of the production values was Warner Brothers' *42nd Street,* which synthesized for all time the two competing universes that coexist in musicals: the world of the flesh—the sorrows of work and life—and the world of fantasy, where dreams can and do come true. This is the essence of *42nd Street,* and the emotional core of many of the greatest musicals Hollywood ever produced. It is even implicit in the medium itself: what is film but an illusion?

Warner Brothers was a surprising but also appropriate place for the musical genre to find its beginnings—

surprising because the company had one foot in the financial grave in 1932 and was known primarily for hard-boiled drama, yet appropriate because these very tribulations gave Warner's musical efforts a grounding in reality that made them appealing and popular. The story of *42nd Street* is well known: an ingenue gets her big break in a Broadway show due to the star's accident. The stock characters provide a certain easy familiarity: Warner Baxter is the hardworking, theater-loving director gambling everything on his last big show; Dick Powell is the chorus boy with a heart of gold; Bebe Daniels is the vain and slightly amoral stage star who learns her lesson in humility; and of course Ruby Keeler is the gamine chorine. But the sum is bigger than the parts, and in the end *42nd Street* touches all the bases of production values: compelling narrative, visual originality, and singable tunes.

The art direction on *42nd Street* is by Jack Okey, one of Warner's two top-billed art directors in the thirties (the other was Anton Grot). Okey cut his teeth in typical tough Warner Brothers films like *The Dawn Patrol* (1930) and *I Am a Fugitive from a Chain Gang* (1932) before drawing this first musical assignment from then-Warner's producer Darryl F. Zanuck. His partner for this production was Busby Berkeley, who received credit for creating and staging the dances and ensembles. One suspects that Okey's work is seen largely in the first half of the film, in settings such as the rehearsal stage, with nothing but a trunk and a threadbare curtain for props, or the underfurnished offices of Baxter's producers, while Berkeley's style dominates the fantasy sequences during the big stage numbers that close the movie, "Young and Healthy" and "42nd Street."

The latter number, taking up the final ten minutes of the film and effectively ending it, was Berkeley's first hit, establishing him as the first great choreographer in Hollywood. Yet it is not the dancing that is the center of attention but the way in which he, and presumably director Lloyd Bacon and Okey as well, uses the camera and camera space to open up the simple vaudeville routine until it becomes an entire imaginary social universe of its own. The song begins, innocently enough, with Keeler singing "42nd Street" in front of a closed curtain, which then parts to reveal a standard stage flat. But then the camera begins to move up, and the stage turns into a set with a subway kiosk, an apple vendor, a barber, and a

mounted policeman competing for our attention. By the time gunfire breaks out and a hundred dancers appear holding miniature skyscrapers, we are clearly no longer on a Broadway stage but somewhere inside Keeler's and Baxter's heads at the moment of their triumph, as Keeler and her costar Powell peer out at the audience from atop the human skyscraper.

Curiously, *42nd Street* does not end with this image of success and happiness, but with the more downbeat image of Baxter sitting dejectedly in the alley after the show, listening to the deprecating comments of the first-nighters (they say he would be nothing without Keeler). The ambiguous ending is a hallmark of many Hollywood musicals, as dozens to follow would copy *42nd Street*'s example and leave the audience with an image of something lost as well as gained. Nevertheless, or perhaps as a result of this, *42nd Street* was a tremendous success, inspiring a host of equally dazzling "backstagers" like the *Golddiggers* series, pulling Warner Brothers out of the red, and, most importantly, proving the viability of movie musicals as a revenue-generating genre. With the coast now clear, other studios jumped in—none with more verve and creativity than MGM.

THE LION'S SHARE

The Lion's Share is the title of Bosley Crowther's book about MGM written soon after the end of the Louis B. Mayer era (Mayer resigned in 1951; the book was published in 1957), but it could refer to anything having to do with MGM. It had the most bankable stars, the biggest financial assets, and the top technical talent in the industry. No surprise then that MGM should also turn out the best films, at least in the genre of musicals. MGM excelled in musicals, a handful of which are among the greatest movies ever made.

MGM's musical unit was so good, in fact, that it produced too many films to discuss in detail. A specialized survey would do them justice, but here discretion is necessary if not particularly valorous. The list of MGM films missing from consideration here would make a "best" list of their own: *Meet Me in St. Louis* (1944), *The Harvey Girls* (1946), *Easter Parade* (1948), *Singin' in the Rain* (1952), and *Gigi* (1958). One unifying factor for all MGM musicals—perhaps the principal unifying fac-

MGM art department, c. 1940: emulating the factory work ethic.

Cedric Gibbons, the aesthetic tastemaker of MGM.

tor—is the presence in one capacity or another of one of the great geniuses in Hollywood, Cedric Gibbons.

Gibbons was born in Brooklyn in 1898; both his father and his grandfather were architects. Naturally, he despised architecture and studied painting at the Art Students League in New York. When he began designing films for Cecil B. DeMille, he was still only in his early twenties. Gibbons was evidently an ambitious as well as a talented young man, for by the time he was twenty-five he was already the head of the art department for Samuel Goldwyn's company. When Goldwyn merged with Metro Pictures in 1924 to form MGM, Gibbons came aboard. From that day until the day he retired in 1956, every MGM picture was contractually obligated to list Gibbons as the art director.

Gibbons enjoyed the royal aspect of Hollywood. He courted publicity and loved to be photographed. He also liked expensive clothes, beautiful women, and exotic foods. He understood the nature of his power, and hired the finest architects, sketch artists, set decorators, and scene painters to work in his department, training them and then promoting them through his influence to important assignments at MGM and eventually at other studios. Gibbons may not have been the single greatest art director in Hollywood history, since too much of his work was executive and administrative as opposed to purely creative, but he was certainly the most influential.

Because Gibbons's career spanned nearly the entire

The Great Ziegfeld (1936)

During the musical numbers, Adrian's exotic costumes often upstage the sets by Cedric Gibbons and John Harkrider. (MGM)

history of MGM, his work is not easily summarized by discussing individual films (though that is still useful). His greatest contributions were ubiquitous: he set the tone for MGM and was largely responsible for the lavish style and meticulous attention to detail that have come to characterize all of MGM's productions, especially the musicals. His influence as a teacher and mentor was profound. Vincente Minnelli began his career working for Gibbons; as much of Gibbons's style wore off on the master director as it did on two of the great art directors of the forties and fifties, Preston Ames and Jack Martin Smith.

THE GREAT ZIEGFELD

It was inevitable that Cedric Gibbons, who considered himself the greatest showman of the movies, would be attracted to the story of Florenz Ziegfeld, the greatest showman of the stage. As was his habit, Gibbons supervised the art department and delegated to his associates the actual task of designing *The Great Ziegfeld* (1936), in this case giving the assignment to Merrill Pye, John Harkrider, and Edwin B. Willis. Harkrider had the ex-

ABOVE: *The Great Ziegfeld*

Set still, the interior of the Sixty Club—
thirties elegance, Gibbons style. (MGM)

INSET: *The Great Ziegfeld*

The film opens with the "Streets of Cairo"
sequence. The property department's
rental list for this scene alone calls for
help from seven different companies,
including two rival studios. (MGM)

LEFT: *The Great Ziegfeld*

A set decorator's nightmare: Billie Burke
(Myrna Loy) and Florenz Ziegfeld
(William Powell) celebrate a modest
Christmas at home.

traordinary good fortune to have actually worked with Ziegfeld, and his input as to the accuracy of the details of the production numbers was invaluable, giving *The Great Ziegfeld* the patina of legitimacy that most movie biographies often lack. Still, it was only a patina. Certainly Gibbons wasn't going to let mere reality interfere with his vision of Ziegfeldian opulence, just as scriptwriter William Anthony McGuire, probably at the insistence of producer Hunt Stromberg, wasn't going to allow biographical fact to interfere with the usual MGM flair for telling a good story.

The standard MGM process for set decoration (accounts that appear over and over again in the memoirs and oral histories) involved a complicated ritual of checks and counterchecks beginning and ending on Gibbons's desk. Gibbons would become involved very early, around the time of the first draft of the screenplay. His sketches and ideas would get passed along to the unit art director, who would hand them out to the sketch artists and then back to Gibbons. He approved them and returned them to the unit man, who would then send them off to be converted into blueprints for the construction department, then back to Gibbons again, and so on. Obviously this kind of game was both costly and time-consuming, which is why MGM histories are littered with huge budgets, accounts of all-night construction parties and of sets being broken down and reused within the hour.

The work shows on the screen. The opening scene of *The Great Ziegfeld* is a little visual model of how Hollywood creates convincing spaces. It is 1893; we are at the World's Columbian Exposition, as created on an MGM sound stage. A small fairground has been built, with a Ferris wheel and the "Streets of Cairo" most visible, lit by perhaps one thousand tiny incandescent bulbs. A crane shot establishes the place and date and moves in over the crowd, allowing us to absorb the atmosphere and the sounds of the fair before skimming down to end with a close-up of Ziegfeld (William Powell) and his attraction, Sandow, the world's strongest man. Without a line of dialogue or exposition, the world of this particular film and of all the characters who will inhabit it is fully explicated.

Every set in *The Great Ziegfeld* is decorated with the same exquisite attention to detail and lit and filmed with the same sensuality as this opening sequence in

Chicago. At one point we see Anna Held (Luise Rainer) rehearsing in her hotel room, and the camera lingers on the vases, decorated piano, white-paneled walls, porcelain figurines, and French mirror as if it longs to stay. We understand Held's tastes and needs as clearly as if she had stopped to tell them to us.

Yet it is the musical sequences, after all, that are the raison d'être for the film and that lift it above the level of the standard prestige MGM production into that of a masterpiece. The musical sequences in *The Great Ziegfeld* are probably the purest examples of Gibbons's own visual style, before he depended entirely on intermediaries to make all the important decisions. Again, Gibbons probably felt a kinship to Ziegfeld. After all, when William Powell as Ziegfeld says, "I want to do a show with silk drapes, with lace, with beautiful girls," he sounds just like a man after Gibbons's own heart.

The most famous musical number in *The Great Ziegfeld* is "A Pretty Girl Is Like a Melody." It begins conventionally, with Dennis Morgan (dubbed by Allan Jones) singing in front of the curtain, but when the curtain goes up all reality lifts away with it. Upon a stage that seems to revolve forever (the sequence actually lasts only ten minutes) there appear rows of girls dressed in frills, a made-up Pagliacci singing an aria, a dozen couples performing a waltz, then an equal number of concert pianists pounding out "Rhapsody in Blue," masked women in bizarre black headpieces dancing a Nazimova-like tarantella, and finally Morgan and company on top of a huge wedding cake that turns out to be the revolving stage. It's all dizzying and spectacular and just a little over the top, perfect for Gibbons—and, incidentally, for Ziegfeld too.

This would have been sufficient, but *The Great Ziegfeld* has over an hour to go, with more elaborately constructed musical numbers (though none quite as outrageous) and more generous, warm interiors, until by the time Ziegfeld dies, in front of a window revealing his own theater, we feel as if we've lived as long as he and we're almost relieved that it is over.

THE WIZARD OF OZ

When *The Wizard of Oz* (1939) went into production, Cedric Gibbons assigned the art direction to William A.

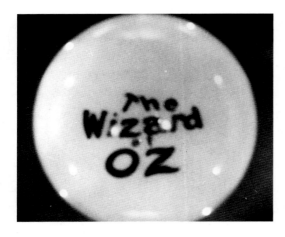

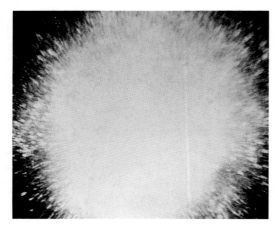

The Wizard of Oz (1939)

The special effects, created by A. Arnold Gillespie, are balanced by the down-to-earth style of the cast and a heartwarming story. The original title sequence, not used in the film, showed the name of the picture written in smoke on the surface of a glass bubble, disappearing when the bubble explodes. (MGM)

Horning. Horning's previous credits in dramas such as *Fury* (1936) and *Marie Antoinette* (1938) gave no hint of his ability to deal with a musical fantasy, but his no-nonsense, budget-conscious working style would come in handy in a production that everyone at the studio knew was going to cost millions of dollars.

Horning joined a production team that was none-too-finely drilled. The musical numbers, written by E. Y. Harburg and Harold Arlen, were largely in place, but everything else, from the cast to the director, changed from meeting to meeting. Producer Arthur Freed had eleven people working on the screenplay at one time or another. This was unusual for the usually seamless MGM organization, and probably reflected in part the studio's nervousness about producing a costly musical without a proven audience—not to mention its awareness of the problems to be surmounted: midgets had to sing and dance, monkeys fly, and animals talk.

Another unproven element certain to raise the temperature of MGM executives was that the middle, fantasy sequences of *The Wizard of Oz* were to be filmed in Technicolor, then a new and still experimental color-film technique. Technicolor was a complicated process, and the parent company required a color consultant to be on the set making sure the cinematographers knew how to run the equipment. Technicolor also brought an entire new series of challenges to art directors, since certain colors (like blue) did not register properly, and others (like yellow and red) had to be toned down so as not to distract from the action. All this uncertainty made *The Wizard of Oz* a chancy production right from the start.

The usual number of sets constructed for a major MGM production in the late thirties was anywhere from thirty-five to fifty; *The Wizard of Oz* required nearly sixty sets, plus the special effects. The art department used almost a third of a mile of cloth for the backdrops. (Some of these were painted by the great Ben Carré, repeating the tasks he had performed for the Paris Opera and silent-film director Maurice Tourneur twenty-five years earlier.) Over one hundred and fifty painters worked around the clock preparing the sets, led by George Gibson, head of the Scenic Art Department, who would perform even greater miracles for *An American in Paris* twelve years later.

The success of the film is a testament to the studio's talent and tenacity. The story progresses without any

The Wizard of Oz

A. Arnold Gillespie cleverly disguised a giant wind sock,
transformed forever into a terrifying cyclone. (MGM)

ABOVE: *The Wizard of Oz*

A production assistant hammers down the final piece of a forest of artificial trees. (MGM)

RIGHT: *The Wizard of Oz*

Scale and continuity were guaranteed by reams of carefully arranged and labeled set stills such as this. (MGM)

OPPOSITE, INSET: *The Wizard of Oz*

A live actor and a puppeteer's strings create the illusion of a talking, gesticulating tree. (MGM)

unintended distractions; the music and A. Arnold Gillespie's special effects propel the characters from one dramatic situation to another, and the casting is perfect. All the performers—especially Jack Haley as the Tin Man, Bert Lahr as the Cowardly Lion, and Ray Bolger as the Scarecrow—make the scenery look normal. These three actors' background in vaudeville and the theatrical traditions associated with it helped them to play with the 10-foot flowers, rubber trees, and winged monkeys as if they were everyday objects.

Horning reserved his most detailed work for the two scenes where it would be most noticed: the arrival of Dorothy in Munchkinland and the arrival of the four friends in Oz. In both cases, the actors allow us to see their character's wonderment at their surroundings, priming us to share their feelings. As Dorothy (Judy Garland) and Toto arrive in Munchkinland, the film switches from black-and-white to Technicolor. Dorothy opens the door of her house and finds herself in a strange land with very large flowers, Dutch-style cottages, and an endless expanse of painted blue hills and valleys. The Munchkins themselves, when they finally appear, seem as much a part of the decor as the houses—we agree instantly with Dorothy when she says, "I don't think we're in Kansas anymore." Everything is oversized to make the people seem smaller; Garland herself is supposed to be a little girl.

By Oz, both Dorothy and the audience have grown a bit more sophisticated, and the Emerald City itself, with its riot of green and Art Deco ornaments, seems like a magical ballroom. Although most adult memories would proclaim Oz to be a busy place indeed, the floor of the "city" is actually virtually bare. The only visual details competing with the four actors as they ride through the square in their carriage drawn by horses of changing colors are a few light stanchions against the wall and several pots of artificial flowers.

The Wizard of Oz is, of course, much more than the sum of its sets. However, it should not be overlooked that in a musical that required a particularly subtle distinction between fantasy and reality, the transformations between the two realms came about almost entirely through the resources of the MGM art department. Each major scene in the film ends with an effect: Dorothy climbs aboard a tornado, the Wicked Witch (Margaret Hamilton) disappears in a fire bomb, the Wizard (Frank

The Wizard of Oz

A production still of the Witch's Castle, with another great matte painting providing the background. (MGM)

Morgan) is first seen as a projection, and eventually the Witch melts and Dorothy returns to Kansas through a combination of wishful thinking and projection. The art direction is a narrative element. And in the end the happy ending is not entirely happy. As she exclaims, "There's no place like home," Dorothy somehow suspects that she—like us—will never recover the innocence that allowed her to visit Oz and meet such wonderful friends.

AN AMERICAN IN PARIS

In 1939 Arthur Freed and his "Freed Unit," as the musical wing of MGM came to be labeled, was just getting started. A little over ten years later, with *Meet Me in St. Louis* and *Singin' in the Rain* behind them, Freed's team—variously including director Vincente Minnelli, actors Gene Kelly and Judy Garland, associate producer Roger Edens, and Cedric Gibbons and his acolytes Preston Ames and Jack Martin Smith—was at the very top of its form. The proof: *An American in Paris* (1951), one of the greatest films Hollywood has ever produced. Its Academy Award–winning production design is probably

the greatest single achievement in art direction in film history.

There are a number of factors that contributed to the overwhelming success of the art direction in *An American in Paris*. First, through lucky happenstance, the picture is about an artist, allowing the visual imaginations of the design team free reign to create sets that are aesthetically pleasing, unique as opposed to clichéd, and in character. Additionally, *An American in Paris* is an original musical, created for the screen and thus free of the usual preconceptions that accompany an adaptation from another source. (Although arguably George Gershwin's score is the source, it is a musical, not a visual, source and suggested no imagery except the locale.) Ames and his design team had the advantage of the extraordinarily collaborative atmosphere that pervaded the production. Ames was hired because he had studied painting in Paris in the twenties; Kelly was not only an actor but the choreographer, and costume designer Irene Sharaff was allowed to help design some of the settings.

An American in Paris is a sophisticated example of the relationship between flesh and fantasy in the Hollywood musical. Each of the major characters in the film has a fantasy: Jerry (Gene Kelly) to be a famous painter,

ABOVE: *An American in Paris*

A set still for the "yellow" sequence in Leslie Caron's introduction. (MGM)

RIGHT: *An American in Paris*

A lamp-laden MGM cart vies for cobblestone space with a pair of Parisian flower carts and a very in-character extra in this casual production still. (MGM)

OPPOSITE, ABOVE: *An American in Paris*

The fantasy ballet: Jerry (Gene Kelly) and Lise (Leslie Caron) do a soft-shoe routine amid a Rousseau-like provincial French town. (MGM)

OPPOSITE, INSET: *An American in Paris*

The fantasy ballet: Lise Bouvier (Leslie Caron) and Jerry Mulligan (Gene Kelly) dance à la Toulouse-Lautrec under a canopy of painted van Gogh stars. (MGM)

BELOW: *An American in Paris*

Painted Paris. (MGM)

Adam (Oscar Levant) to be a concert pianist, Milo (Nina Foch) to be the sponsor of an undiscovered genius, and Lise (Leslie Caron) to fall in love deeply and completely. Each, in turn, gets tested by being granted his or her fantasy as reality, and accepting it or rejecting it according to how true it actually feels.

Ames's art direction continually comments on this tug-of-war between fantasy and reality. The biggest fantasy, of course, is the setting itself: except for the opening montage of the Champs Elysées, the Place de la République, and the Seine, not one foot of the film was actually shot in Paris. (One MGM lot was so meticulously tricked out in red, white, and blue and so realistic that the elderly artist Raoul Dufy reportedly wept when Kelly arranged a special screening for him.) The scene where Kelly and Caron dance on the Left Bank was designed by George Gibson with a scenic background of Notre Dame and a bridge painted in, the lights dimmed to make it look like night, and the focus continually kept on the young lovers. MGM technicians lay off-camera, paddling the three-inch-deep "Seine" to make it look like a flowing river.

Again and again, examples of Ames's wizardry astound the careful viewer. When Georges Guetary sings "Stairway to Paradise," the steps of the stairway light up as he touches each one with his feet. To increase the illusion of depth outside Jerry's studio, Ames built scale models of the rooftops and chimneys of Paris and inserted them in front of the painted background of Montmartre. Every detail, from the rigging on the carriages to the stems on the champagne glasses, was designed to be completely accurate.

The climax of all this, both for the story in the film and for its art direction, is the seventeen-minute ballet with which the production concludes. Having conceded that Lise will never love him, Jerry has given himself to Milo and the two of them attend a black-and-white artists' ball. In a room full of mad revelers (dressed, of course, only in outrageous black-and-white costumes), Jerry tries one last time to woo Lise and fails; he leaves the party to get some air on the balcony. There, overlooking the Paris that was the source of all his hopes and equally of all his failures, Jerry begins to sketch. The sketch turns into a set, which in contrast to the dazzling but relentless black-and-white of the ball is in blazing tricolor—red, white, and blue.

The number, according to Ames (as quoted by Donald Knox in *The Magic Factory*), was intended from the start to be "a ballet about painters." Kelly worked on the choreography and danced (of course) to Gershwin's "An American in Paris," while Ames and Gibson painted backdrops in the styles of various modern French artists. Ames apparently is responsible for the first setting, a panoramic view of the Place de la Concorde in the style of Dufy, with a plaster-cast fountain designed by the head of the plaster shop, Henry Greutert. It was, in Gibson's words, "as much Dufy as you could make a three-dimensional object."

Gibson himself created the other settings of the ballet—the flower market in the style of Auguste Renoir, Montmartre as seen by Maurice Utrillo, Henri Rousseau-like fairgrounds, the Place de l'Opéra by Vincent van Gogh, and a Toulouse-Lautrec bar. Gibson has explained how the "happy accidents" of the test sketches were so beautiful that it was decided to duplicate them on the set exactly to scale—250 feet wide and 35 to 40 feet high. Apparently both Kelly and Sharaff also contributed to the production design for the ballet fantasy due to its extreme complexity.

All fantasies must come to an end, "An American in Paris" (the ballet) among them, but in this case *An American in Paris* (the movie) has a happy ending as well, as Jerry awakens from his dream on the balcony to see Lise returning to him with his rival's blessing. The sorrowful aspects of the musical—Milo's loneliness and Adam's failure—are pushed to the side, and the last image of the film is that of Gene Kelly and Leslie Caron embracing as the camera pulls back from them and over a long shot of that beautiful and star-lit sound stage they called Paris.

FROM STAGE TO SCREEN

The stereotypical image of the Hollywood musical, straight out of a Fred Astaire movie, is that of an elegantly dressed couple sweeping across the dance floor of a posh Manhattan nightclub. In reality, there are many kinds of Hollywood musicals, and each requires a different approach to its settings.

"Backstagers," such as *42nd Street,* are the cheapest musicals to produce and require little more than an empty and available theater. Fantasies like *The Wizard of Oz* are costly and risky, but when successful they can be rewarding. *Meet Me in St. Louis* and *Easter Parade* are period dramas with music, and the accuracy of the costumes and the scenery were the art department's primary concerns. Even the Marx Brothers got into the act; although no one could call *Horsefeathers* (1932) or *Duck Soup* (1933) musicals, Groucho and company sing several numbers. It is thus difficult to make generalizations under the rubric "musicals," because the integration of song into the drama can be accomplished in so many different ways.

In the fifties, the predominant musical genre was the screen adaptation. One reason for this was the increased competition the industry faced from television. The motto was In times of trouble, grab a sure thing. A Broadway hit was a proven commodity with hummable tunes. In addition, the fifties were the heyday of the book musical, one heavy with plot and with a strong dramatic story capable of propelling the action and involving the audience in a more intimate manner than the previous decades' revue-based shows or musical biographies.

The biggest problem facing the art director in a musical adaptation of a Broadway show is to discover the proper manner of translating the two-dimensional characteristics of a musical number into the three-dimensional nature of a film drama. To film the entire production on location would prove too costly, let alone look ridiculous, while a completely studio-bound production might render the sensitive story line completely limp. The most successful musical adaptations of the past forty years have either separated their music from the story entirely (as in Bob Fosse's *Cabaret,* 1972) or recast the entire production as a fantasy (*The Rocky Horror Picture Show,* 1975).

Somewhere between these two extremes lie *Carousel* and *West Side Story.* Both these shows, despite their exuberant and lovely scores, are essentially tragedies, and both opt for an uneasy and at times deliberately disconcerting blend of fantasy and startling reality. *Carousel* is the preeminent example of art direction in a Rodgers and Hammerstein film production (not counting *The Sound of Music,* 1965, which cheated by shooting in the Austrian Alps), and *West Side Story* remains the most honored film in Academy Award history (it won

*An unreal setting for an unreal world:
the fairway of a traveling carnival, turn-
of-the-century Maine. (Universal)*

twelve, including one for its art director, Boris Leven).

The settings for *Carousel* (1956) were principally
the work of Jack Martin Smith. Smith began his career at
MGM, working uncredited on *The Wizard of Oz,* then
blossoming in his collaborations with Vincente Minnelli
on *Meet Me in St. Louis, Yolanda and the Thief*
(1945), and *The Pirate* (1948). In 1955 he moved to
20th Century-Fox to work for Lyle Wheeler, who had
skipped out of MGM ten years earlier to become Fox's
supervisory art director when Richard Day left for Goldwyn. (Like star athletes, star art directors changed
teams often.) In later years Smith worked in projects as
varied as the "Batman" television series (1965–68),
where he designed the infamous Pop art sets, and big,
old-fashioned productions like *Tora! Tora! Tora!* (1970).

Carousel begins with the hero, Billy Bigelow (Gordon MacRae), already dead and in heaven. He's sitting
on a stool, polishing a clear plastic star. Smith's vision of
heaven is not unlike a very efficient minimum-security
prison camp in a heavy fog—the details are hard to see
and nobody seems especially happy. MacRae gets called
into the Starkeeper's office (which is furnished like an
accountant's office with see-through walls) and there
reminisces about the events that put him in his cloudy
abode. Having adjusted to this abstract scene, the audience is thrust firmly down to earth, to a sunny day at a
Maine fairground sometime around the turn of the century.

The earthly settings of *Carousel* do not seem quite
the period pieces we expect them to be. The reason for
this is that Smith and the director, Henry King, envisioned the pastoral New England landscape as being as
much an abstract location as heaven. Billy sings his
"Soliloquy" amid a setting of rocks and sea. In the
"Carousel Ballet," Jacques d'Amboise and Susan Luckey
as Louise dance in the sand. With settings like these, or
even slightly more complex ones like the shack that Billy
and Julie (Shirley Jones) live in, Smith emphasizes the
mythic aspect of this small Maine seaport and how much
the characters' lives are tied to the earth and the sea.
Julie and Louise, in particular, are elemental in their driving passions and simple faith. By couching the real in
such symbolic terms, the more overtly symbolic settings,
such as the Starkeeper's office, do not seem so strange.

In contrast, the film's big production numbers, "June
Is Bustin' Out All Over" and "A Real Nice Clambake,"
come across as stage bound, and the considerable charm
that emerges from them is principally due to the ener-
getic camera work and costumes, rather than the ordinary locations chosen for their settings. Despite these
happy musical numbers, *Carousel* remains basically a

West Side Story (1961)

*Except for a slight change in the room's archi-
tecture, the setting for the dance in the completed film mimics Boris Leven's original sketch in
every detail. (Columbia)*

OPPOSITE: *West Side Story*

*Tony (Richard Beymer) and Maria (Natalie
Wood) share a loving moment from within the
confines of their symbolic cages. (Columbia)*

tragedy, ending with the lovers separated forever (he's used up his quota of one return visit). Julie casts a longing look toward the sea and Billy fades into the sunset on a blank expanse of beach.

West Side Story (1961) is more purely a tragedy, based as it is on one of the great tragedies of all time, *Romeo and Juliet.* The original musical, with music by

Leonard Bernstein and lyrics by Stephen Sondheim, was a big hit, but the movie put the show through the roof, becoming an instant classic and turning several of its songs into standards—this despite innumerable obstacles, the principal one being the fact that the two leads, Richard Beymer as Tony and Natalie Wood as Maria, were miscast and couldn't sing. Their voices were dubbed, but the story is so compelling and the music so beautiful that no one really noticed.

In this mission to translate the story of the doomed young lovers caught in a gang war in New York, directors Robert Wise and Jerome Robbins (Robbins was fired shortly into production) receive considerable help from their art director, Boris Leven. Leven had been designing films in Hollywood for over twenty years without attracting much attention when he drew the *West Side Story* assignment. He and Wise must have found their niche, for after this they went on to do excellent work together in *The Sound of Music* (1965) and *Star!* (1968).

West Side Story opted for constructed sets in every scene except for the opening montage of city landmarks (in this way it exactly parallels *An American in Paris*), and this heightened realism adds to the emotional charge of the story. The walls are layered with graffiti, the narrow alleys are clogged with garbage and rubble, and the storefronts are empty and abandoned. Although the rival gangs range across the streets and basketball courts of their neighborhood with the finesse of highly trained dancers (which is, after all, what they are), Leven creates constant reminders that their playground

is also their prison. The first gang brawl is staged on one of the ball courts, and the chain-link fence that towers over all of them and inhibits their freedom and escape uncannily resembles the fence of a cellblock.

Even the hopeful characters in the story are trapped by the settings that define their universe. Maria works in the back room of a dress shop without windows; all she has to look at is a brick wall. And Tony must hide in the basement of Doc's drugstore, a prisoner even at the last moment of his chance for freedom, a chance that Leven's sets tell us is doomed from the start. Their mock wedding, staged in the storeroom of the dress shop as they sing "One Hand, One Heart," is witnessed by nothing more human than a clothes dummy.

The conceit of doomed prisoners is completed at the end of the movie. Tony, imagining that Maria is dead, has foolishly run out into the open spaces of the playground to challenge her alleged murderer, Chino. Rattling the chains of his cell, the fence, in one last gasp of freedom, he shouts out Chino's name, only to see Maria alive, after all. But before he can reach her and run away, Chino indeed finds Tony and shoots him. In a circle of light thrown by a streetlamp but not unlike the accusatory searchlight of a prison yard, Maria cradles Tony's body and curses all the Sharks and Jets for killing her love with their hatred. Chastened, the gang members slowly march out of the playground in single file, like prisoners returning to their cells. The camera pulls up and back to reveal the real prison they are all in—New York, with its poverty and struggles.

After *West Side Story,* the Hollywood musical sputtered on, the occasional flashes of brilliance illuminating a greater amount of ennui. *The Sound of Music* and *Mary Poppins* (1964) were lovely and charming, but atypical. More telling were ill-fated attempts to capture Hollywood's past with musical travesties such as *Lost Horizon* (1973) and *At Long Last Love* (1975). The genre was dead. Popular music filled the gap uneasily, generating soundtracks like that of *Saturday Night Fever* (1977), which were memorable but not truly musicals. Fosse's *Cabaret,* with its sinister message and German design team, was the last truly great musical adaptation. The careful balance between flesh and fantasy had unraveled; there is all too much flesh and little confidence in fantasy. From the uncertain present, the past seems very appealing indeed.

THE WITHERED HEATH: CLASSIC HORROR FILMS

The iconography of horror—with its shadowy abodes, moonlit landscapes, and monsters—has become so familiar that it is somewhat surprising to learn that the convention is barely one hundred years old. Bram Stoker's *Dracula*, written in 1897, was the first modern horror story, though intimations of the genre are found earlier in Mary Shelley's *Frankenstein* and Victorian penny dreadfuls such as *Camilla* and *Varney the Vampire*. The imagery in the film version of *Dracula* (1931), for instance, did not spring to life fully born. Its visual elements were borrowed from diverse sources—literary ones like Stoker and Shelley, theatrical effects from the stage, and such silent movies as *The Cabinet of Dr. Caligari* (1919), with its visual distortion as a psychological metaphor; *The Golem* (1920), with man-made monsters; and *Metropolis* (1926), which showed the evils of technology. Add to this the age-old conflict between rich and poor (idle barons inflicting their will upon innocent peasants) and authority versus freedom (unfeeling police interfering with the genius of science), and all the necessary ingredients for a classic concoction are in place.

Not considered as classy as musicals, nor as serious as dramas, horror films traditionally received the smallest budgets

Dracula (1931) *Count Dracula's brides-in-waiting. Charles D. Hall never wasted an opportunity to include immense, sculpted mantelpieces and paneled picture windows in his Gothic mansions. (Universal)*

and little star support. Ironically, these so-called deprivations in many cases actually improved the films, and today these once-poor sisters of the "prestige" productions are viewed with respect and admiration for their artistic qualities.

UNIVERSAL'S MONSTERS

Carl Laemmle is the grandfather of the horror film. As the head of Universal Pictures, a small, independent studio, he had the Frankenstein-like power to create anything he chose. His childhood in Germany was filled with tales of the Black Forest and of evil doings in the castles in the mountains. When his son, Carl Laemmle, Jr., took over the studio in 1930 and attempted to compete with the major studios, Universal produced three great horror films: *Dracula, The Bride of Frankenstein,* and *The Invisible Man.*

The man responsible for the art direction on all three films was Charles D. Hall. His career spanned five decades, almost all of them for Universal. Some of his creations have become so common they are now clichés, such as the mad scientist's laboratory or the Tudor village with its torch-bearing peasants. Yet his value to the studio and the genre for which it is most famous has been generally overlooked—an eight-hundred-page history of Universal fails to mention his name even once. Along with makeup director Jack Pierce and special-effects master John P. Fulton, Hall led Universal Pictures through a decade of classic horror movies that remain unsurpassed for their visual power to fascinate and frighten.

Although *Dracula* was the first, it is in many ways the weakest of Universal's prestige horror productions. Director Tod Browning basically restaged the Broadway play on which the film is based, and there is little camera

OPPOSITE: *Dracula*

Count Dracula (Bela Lugosi) and his latest victim. The film's art director, Charles D. Hall, can rightly be claimed as the inventor of the attributes of the horror genre. Dracula has the first cobwebbed stairs, the first ruined house, the first blasted tree, and the first rifled crypt. (Universal)

work or music to enhance the story. Despite these shortcomings, *Dracula* contains some purely visual elements that capture the essence of Hall's work and bring a mood of foreboding to the picture. There is the Eastern European village that Renfield first visits, its thatched hut containing a cast-iron caldron simmering over a fire and a rocking chair decorated with folk-art designs. Or Dracula's castle, a shambles of baronial nobility with crumbling walls and cobwebs elegantly stretched along its corners.

It isn't until nearly halfway through the film that we see the first fully lit set: Lucy Seward's apartment on the sanitarium grounds. Her place is strangely up-to-date, the furnishings much more reminiscent of the 1930s, when the film was made, than the 1890s, during which the story is supposedly taking place. But this fits in with the different levels of morality with which Hall has invested his architectural settings—contemporary being the most heavenly; rustic neither good nor bad, like purgatory; and High Gothic being the most evil. This original cosmology was probably a result of Hall's and Universal's tacit sympathy with the prevailing architectural currents, which claimed as gospel the preeminence of modernism. In addition, there is a lot of religious symbolism in the settings. Dracula (Bela Lugosi) dies in a vaulted crypt and crosses appear everywhere. The film ends with Mina and Jonathan climbing out of the crypt and into the light, while church bells ring repeatedly on the soundtrack.

At times Hall's primitive designs work for him, such as in the first scene in London, where the stage fog obscures the entire set save for one pillar, or the scene with Renfield in his room in the sanitarium, suggested entirely by a bed and his exaggerated shadow on the bare, white wall. Partially, of course, this is making a virtue out of necessity, since Universal could never afford to build sets as large or complex as those of MGM. But there remains the feeling that a big budget would not improve *Dracula* and that certain things are better off half-seen.

Frankenstein (1931) was in production before *Dracula* was released, so Carl Laemmle, Jr., could not have known he was fashioning a new and popular genre—the first of the half-dozen Frankenstein films Universal launched upon an eager public in the next ten years. *Frankenstein* was a vast improvement upon *Dracula,* and *The Bride of Frankenstein* (1935), the first sequel, an improvement upon an improvement.

OPPOSITE, INSET: *Frankenstein* (1931)

Charles D. Hall's Middle European village was used first in Frankenstein *and again in all the Universal sequels. (Universal)*

LEFT: *The Bride of Frankenstein*

The Frankenstein *set, slightly redressed to appear a bit more Tudor. (Universal)*

Both films—and *The Invisible Man* (1933)—share not only Hall's increasingly sophisticated art direction but the expert light touch of director James Whale. He brought the right combination of the horrific and high camp to his productions to allow them to work as safe-for-children horror movies as well as highly entertaining fare for adults. These qualities helped them to survive and flourish.

The Bride of Frankenstein is far from a mindless and illogical sequel of the original. Whale has added Frankenstein's delightfully demented mentor, Dr. Praetorius (played for humor by Ernest Thesiger) and several side plots like that of the monster and the hermit that have become familiar through their parody in Mel Brooks's *Young Frankenstein* (1974). To suit a movie that is serious but none too grave, Hall pulled out all the tricks in his book of horror-film designs, from the *Caligari*-like distorted walls and stairwell of Dr. Praetorius's "humble abode" to Frankenstein's castle, with its drawbridge, stone turrets, sticks of rough-hewn but fashionable furniture, and canopied bed. There is a wonderfully abstract forest, with casually placed trees nearly bare of branches that mimic and mock the monster's own vertical, graceless nature. The monster's flight through this cinematic Garden of Gethsemane ends with him caught and bound to a felled tree, hoisted above the crowd like Christ. The designs are occasionally incongruous. At one point, the village, which seemed squarely Middle European, appears to be Tudor in an establishing shot with

The Bride of Frankenstein

The classic Charles D. Hall fire-place and paneled window, this time augmented by Gothic vault-ing. Baron Frankenstein (Colin Clive) lounges in his mammoth bed, which features a carved Baroque headboard and a 20-foot-high funneled canopy. (Universal)

BELOW:
The Bride of Frankenstein

The monster (Boris Karloff) as Christ, in a blasted Gethsemane. (Universal)

the monster fleeing down the street. There's even a Tudor-like apartment building in the distance.

The most famous set in *The Bride of Frankenstein* is the electrical tower where Frankenstein (Colin Clive) and Praetorius create the monster's mate. Retained from *Frankenstein,* this room was designed by Hall in collaboration with Herman Rosse, one of Laemmle's associates from the early days in Germany, with electrical props by Kenneth Strickfaden, by profession an engineer. The efficacy of the set is enhanced by Franz Waxman's brooding score and by John Mescall's propensity for tilting the camera 45 degrees backward throughout the scene, adding the element of displacement to an already existing chaos. In between the flying wires, Art Deco–style mobiles, trilevel kites, bursting smoke bombs, and showers of sparks, the bride's body is lifted to heaven to receive God's gift of life. All fails, of course. Boris Karloff, as the monster, mutters the immortal line: "We belong dead," and the set collapses into ruins for all time, or at least until it was needed for *Son of Frankenstein* in 1939.

Hall's masterpiece, and perhaps the greatest horror film Universal ever made, is *The Invisible Man,* again directed by Whale and designed by Hall. *The Invisible Man* is of a piece, so far as mood and decor are concerned, with the studio's other horrific stories. H. G. Wells was a fertile source for Hollywood; he was the author of the novel on which *The Invisible Man* was based as well as the novels *The Shape of Things to Come* and *The War of the Worlds,* which were turned into classic science-fiction films.

The Invisible Man begins, as do *Dracula* and *The Bride of Frankenstein,* with the "monster" fully formed and the innocent already imperiled without their knowledge. In this case, the "monster" is Dr. Jack Griffin (Claude Rains), who has conducted an experiment on himself that has rendered him invisible. The innocent

The Bride of Frankenstein (1935)

At his best, Charles D. Hall created sets that capture the poetry of loneliness. None is more poignant than this mute testament to the inevitability of death. (Universal)

ABOVE:
The Bride of Frankenstein

The original laboratory set from
Frankenstein, *designed by Charles
D. Hall, Herman Rosse, and Kenneth Strickfaden, rejuvenated for
the birth of the bride. (Universal)*

OPPOSITE, ABOVE:
Son of Frankenstein (1939)

*Sketch by Universal art direc-
tor Jack Otterson for the
library in the Frankenstein
castle. (Universal)*

OPPOSITE, BELOW:
Son of Frankenstein

*Sketch by Universal art director
Jack Otterson for the burgomas-
ter's home. (Universal)*

include his beloved Mary and the towns-people of Ipping, the small village to which Griffin has retreated in an attempt to reverse the experiment and rematerialize.

The film opens in a snowstorm, as the heavily bandaged and wrapped doctor struggles into Ipping and takes a room at the Lion's Head Inn. The comfortable setting of the inn, with its sturdy wooden floor and benches, its fire and dart board, and its friendly, chatting patrons, is a direct challenge to the irritable, demanding, and of course mysteriously bandaged man. The juxtaposition of the known versus the unknown and the crowd versus the individual are the hallmarks of Universal's horror style, and Hall has designed sets that represent and dramatize these conflicts in both subtle and obvious ways.

One example is Hall's design of the stairwell leading up to Griffin's lab in the inn. (Hall evidently loved staircases—big, sweeping stone staircases; narrow, twisting metal ones; and heavy, deep wooden ones—and managed to work at least one dramatic sequence involving a staircase into every film.) Here the staircase exaggerates Griffin's feelings of superiority over mere visible men, as evidenced in the scene where, having removed his clothes and bandages, Griffin shoves his way unseen down the steps and through the astonished onlookers. The staircase is also

the scene of the recurring battle between Griffin (his voice, anyway, provided by Rains) and the mistress of the inn, played by the perpetually hysterical Una O'Connor. Another expressive set is the barn in which Griffin meets his ultimate demise. Never one to pass up a religious symbol, Hall and special-effects man John Fulton place the invisible man in a bed of hay, like the Christ child in the manger. As in the opening scene, it is snowing. In order to draw Griffin out, the crowd has set fire to the barn; the coldness of the snow is dissipated by the fire. Griffin may be invisible, but he is not immortal: bullets kill him, and as life departs, Rains gets his first—and only—on-screen appearance in the role.

The smoothness of the continuity and the compelling aspects of the story mask the occasional harmless lapses of logic that Hall often allows in his work. In one scene, early in the film, Griffin's old associate Kemp is hard at work in his laboratory while Griffin's daughter, Flora, looks on. At one point, Flora walks through a doorway into the adjoining room, and the camera pans around to follow her, passing through the nonexistent wall! Later Kemp opens the door to his lab and walks straight out into a forest.

The Invisible Man is a superlative example of Hall's and Fulton's work. The settings and the special effects are so carefully modulated to the tempo of the story and presented in so unforced and natural a manner that they seem almost ordinary, as if any one of us might someday find ourselves invisible and alone. It is this understanding of the ordinary that makes *The Invisible Man* so believable, and that singles out Universal's work as so . . . universal.

ALBERT S. D'AGOSTINO AND THE PSYCHOLOGICAL HORROR FILM

Because of the all-too-real horrors of World War II, the American moviegoing public and the major film studios lost their taste for outright ghoulishness. Instead, taste turned inward, to the hidden fears that terrify us, such as loneliness, frustration, and isolation. The forties and early fifties were the era of the psychological horror film, in which the true terror is not knowing your adversary and any victory is temporary, since the "monster" lurks inside every human and could reappear at any moment.

The master of art direction for the psychological tale of terror was Albert S. d'Agostino, who began his career at MGM and then went to Universal (where he studied with Charles D. Hall). He finally flourished when he went over to work for RKO in 1936, where he stayed for twenty-two years. D'Agostino usually worked with a collaborator, in most cases Walter Keller and set decorator Darrell Silvera. Their films show a remarkable ability to obtain evocative results from a minimal amount of set construction and decoration. Somehow, these everyday settings appear threatening and unyielding. They are casually—even accidentally—thrown into the path of the protagonist or hero.

Early evidence of d'Agostino's abilities came in a trio of movies he designed for producer Val Lewton and director Jacques Tourneur: *Cat People* (1942), *I Walked with a Zombie* (1943), and *The Leopard Man* (also 1943). As the titles reveal, RKO had no qualms about exploiting its films for the maximum potential audience, but in fact the titles are the films' most lurid element; there is considerably less blood and a lot more goose-pimply terror in Lewton's movies than in their haunted-house and monster descendants.

All three films include d'Agostino's characteristically

underlit sets, with only half of the streets and houses visible in the indistinct shadows; all include one classic moment of terror in which the actual horror is never even seen, only implied, an imaginary image superimposed upon a shadow. In *Cat People* it is Irena (Simone Simon) stalking her rival in a pool, where the footfalls of a big cat echo across the alarmingly still water and bare, white tiles. In *I Walked with a Zombie* it is the totally silent sequence of Betsy (Frances Dee) being led through the sugarcane fields on the way to the voodoo ceremony, a moment of bone-chilling anticipation. And in *The Leopard Man* it is the scene where Maria is followed by a leopard, and her murder is overheard by her mother, who has barred the door against her due to her misbehavior and realizes what she has done only when a small trickle of blood begins to seep into the house from beneath the door. D'Agostino's understanding of the terror that lurks in everyday locations, such as a swimming pool, a field, or even your own front door, contributes immensely to the effectiveness of each scene.

As the forties ended and the fifties began, the terror of everyday life in the modern world was abetted by the newfound terrors of UFOs and Communists. These foreign and unknown enemies were often conflated and made convenient foils for an increasingly fractious and morally confused society. They also made excellent subjects for films. Often they came together in an uneasy and now laughable way, such as *Red Planet Mars* (1952), in which the Martians seem to be openly working with the Communists. This film includes the sorry spectacle of production designer Harry Horner trying to direct (he returned quickly to designing) and the sad swan song of the once-great Charles D. Hall. But occasionally the topic of otherworldly beings inspired a masterpiece, and never more so than in *The Thing* (1951).

The Thing (actually titled *The Thing from Another World*) tells the story of a group of scientists and military men camped at the North Pole, trying to defend themselves against a visitor from outer space. Directed by former film editor Christian Nyby with some uncredited help from his producer, Howard Hawks, *The Thing* takes place mainly on one set, the corrugated-steel pole camp, which is the crews' protection and their prison. The conflict in the film is less between man and beast than between men, as the scientists, led by Dr. Carrington (Robert Cornthwaite), argue for preserving the Thing for study, while the Air Force, led by General Hendry (Kenneth Tobey), want the Thing destroyed before it destroys them. Early images of cooperation, such as the moment when the crew forms a circle of outstretched hands on the ice to measure the circumference of the spacecraft, give way to near anarchy, as the men break apart, panic, and die one by one. Eventually central authority and political expediency triumph, as they always do in films made by or for Hawks, but not before ace reporter Ned Scott (Douglas Spencer) warns the audience: "Watch the skies everywhere. Keep looking! Keep watching the skies!" The film ends with a question mark after the words "The End." The indictment of America's lack of vigilance against the menace of Communism could not have been made more clear.

The Thing remains an important film today not because of its dated (though still generally valid) message, but because of the skill of its production. Although barely ninety minutes long, the film has a drive and excitement that today's more elaborate epics rarely capture. Part of this economy comes from the decision of the art directors—d'Agostino and John J. Hughes—to limit the production to six sets—and only one in the last hour: the pole camp. Although cost-cutting decisions were always welcome, this limitation was almost certainly deliberate in an attempt to ground the movie in real time and to give it the feel of a documentary. Thus *The Thing* is an extraordinarily forward-looking film, closer in its effect to the realism to come than to the standard, stagy melodramas of the thirties.

In order to dramatize the atmosphere of greater good that permeates *The Thing,* d'Agostino and Hughes created many claustrophobic settings designed to force the protagonists to sink or swim together. From the men in the airplane on the way to the North Pole, rattling in their cots while the smooth walls of the plane's skin fold over them like a steel-lined coffin, to the passageways in the pole camp, stuffed with wooden oil drums and packing cases, to the layers of leather, cloth, and fur that the men are endlessly pulling off or on to stay comfortable, *The Thing* is filled with images of men enclosed or trapped. And when the heat fails and the battle against the elements turns into a battle against time, the screws that hold these claustrophobic settings together are

turned one notch tighter. Not even Miss Nicholson (Margaret Sheridan), offering coffee to the frozen survivors, helps to relieve the tension, for they never leave the hut, but instead warn us to watch the skies, and so turn the entire world into an enclosed, terrifying, and unsafe place.

MODERN HORROR

With the exception of a few productions of note that reinvent or invert the genre—e.g., *Psycho* (1960) and *Halloween* (1978)—the horror movie in the last thirty years has become increasingly the province of adolescents. The endless procession of blood-spattering heroes like Jason of the *Halloween* sequels and Freddy Krueger of *A Nightmare on Elm Street* have made horror movies the B films of their generation. Needless to say, all these films have production designers, and while their accomplishments are relatively admirable, the level of inventiveness and originality leaves much to be desired when compared with the work of their predecessors.

Perhaps the single greatest advances in art direction for the horror film since 1960 have been technological. As has been the case with so many other aspects of the industry, new technology has allowed art directors and special-effects designers to show us, in explicit detail, horrors that previous generations have only been able to imagine. This can be beneficial to the movie, even if only to add to the sheer spectacle of the production (and to its budget); it is, after all, one of the reasons people go to the movies, especially today, when an "ordinary" movie can be watched on videotape at a fraction of the price.

There are many examples of the new, technology-based horror film (and many, many more in science fiction—more about this later), but perhaps the quintessential one, for the way in which it meets the challenge of combining effects with a strong story, is James Cameron's *Aliens* (1986). As a sequel to the horror film *Alien* (1979), directed by Ridley Scott, *Aliens* had a built-in audience and built-in expectations. However, the production designer for *Aliens,* Peter Lamont, did not work on the earlier film. He inherited a pre-set visual style but dared not repeat *Alien*'s exact look. The result is a fascinating hybrid, borrowing some of the conceits of

Alien and readjusting them to an altogether new and different story.

Veteran production designer Lamont was responsible for almost all of the James Bond films of the sixties and seventies, and thus had at least some familiarity with the charm and the danger of technology. From *Alien*'s production designer, Michael Seymour, Lamont borrowed the idea of making the scenery resemble the aliens, both having long, cablelike extensions and slick surfaces that are halfway between the industrial and the organic. He also inherited H. R. Giger's design of the creatures themselves.

The original *Alien* owed much to *The Thing,* with its tale of an unknown enemy in an isolated location, and Lamont paid homage to both films with his reuse of the claustrophobic pods that the crew sleeps in en route to deep space. He also reused the blue haze that makes the creatures so hard to pick out amid the space rubble aboard the *Nostromo* in *Alien.*

But there are newer elements in *Aliens,* elements that add to the story and separate it from the science-fiction and horror remakes that dominated the eighties. The technology is presented in a matter-of-fact way, not for its own sake but to heighten the irony of the ending, when the battle is reduced to Ripley (Sigourney Weaver) versus the Alien Queen. Lamont and the special-effects team (which included not only Stan Winston, who designed the alien effects, but an entire group of people called the L.A. Effects Group, Inc., and three visual-effects supervisors) built a space station that resembles a cross between an airport and a mall, and designed weapons that are like oversized toys. These effects, so mundane and contrary to expectations, have a surprising way of humanizing the story. By the time it boils down to the inevitable confrontation between the two surrogate mothers—each defending her species—the high-tech wizardry that leads to the firefight does not distract from the will of the two combatants. When Ripley climbs aboard the loading machine and snarls, "Get away from her, you bitch!" it is the up-to-date version of the good and evil Marias of Fritz Lang's *Metropolis* from sixty years earlier—the twin halves of human nature, with good triumphant.

It is reassuring to discover that despite the immense production costs and a running time of nearly three hours, human values in *Aliens* still have the upper hand.

The lesson that Dr. Griffin learned at the end of *The Invisible Man* is still being learned: "I meddled in things that man must leave alone," he said, to which we add, "and no million-dollar budget alone will ever solve."

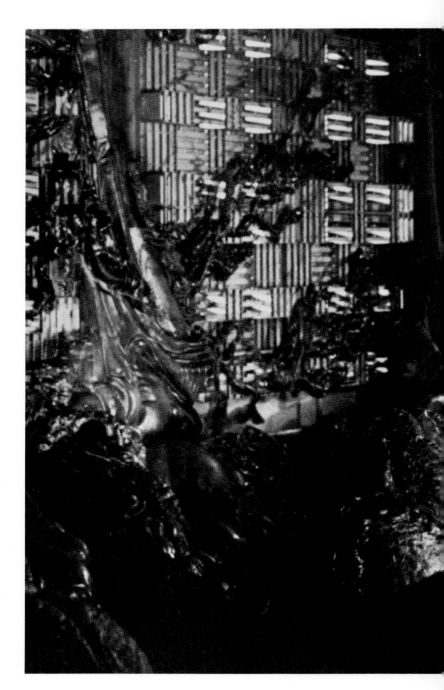

RIGHT: *Aliens* (1986)

The Alien Queen. (Fox)

Aliens Ripley (Sigourney Weaver) with Newt (Carrie Henn) in the aliens' egg nest. (Fox)

THE BIG WHITE SET: MODERN ARCHITECTURE IN THE MOVIES

E very movie has architecture. Period dramas increase their verisimilitude by suggesting the style of the buildings the characters actually would inhabit. Science fiction uses architecture to help convince the viewer of the reality of an imaginary universe. In modern drama, the architectural style is supposed to be unobtrusive; in psychological studies, metaphorical. The art director must confront the role of architecture in designing the settings if the film is to succeed. By closely examining several films in which the architectural details are a critical element of the overall production design, the importance of these details is revealed. Further, one can discern a specific pattern to Hollywood's attitude toward modern architecture, an attitude that moves from outright ridicule to respect of power, and finally to illogical terror. These attitudes, of course, merely reflect our own changing feelings about the buildings around us and their effect upon us.

Hollywood originally turned to architects and designers with architectural training to design sets, believing that knowledge of the multidimensionality of constructed space was a necessary prerequisite to designing for film. D. W. Griffith, Cecil B. DeMille, and Erich von Stroheim all built massive, multistylistic sets, and art directors such as Wilfred Buckland and William Cameron Menzies were valued as much for their the-

atrical knowledge and architectural skills as for their ability to supervise a large production. Eventually, as construction grew more visually sophisticated, "architecture" meant suggestive shapes, partly built spaces, and simplification. Art directors no longer needed to be expert architects; their most important attribute was filmic sense.

DUCK SOUP

The most up-to-date architectural style of the twenties was Art Deco. Derived from the elegant, swirling shapes of late Victorian design and the geometric rigidity of Cubism, Art Deco quickly became extremely popular, particularly in Paris and New York. The Art Deco style was used mostly for interior design—furnishings and decorative objects—rather than for entire buildings. By the time it reached Hollywood around 1930, Art Deco had come to symbolize a generation of freethinking, fun-loving young people who soaked themselves in gin-filled bathtubs and partied all night at glittering nightclubs.

Naturally, such reckless exuberance was ripe for parody, and the unfortunate arrival of the Depression made the target that much juicier. Never mind the fact that Hollywood itself was one of the more flagrant perpe-

trators of decadence: people liked making fun of the rich. And no one made fun of anything with such wicked humor as the Marx Brothers.

Duck Soup (1933) was the Marx Brothers' fifth film for Paramount, whose personal finances were tottering about as severely as the nation's at the time. No one ever knew quite what to do with the Marx Brothers on film, which accounts for the frequent breaking down of continuity or the continual interruptions as Groucho or Harpo improvise bits of old vaudeville business. *Duck Soup* is supposedly the story of two warring nations, Freedonia (of which Groucho has been appointed president) and Sylvania, and of Mrs. Teasdale (the ubiquitous Margaret Dumont) trying to make peace with both sides. But this tells us nothing; God, or at least the God of the Marx Brothers, is in the details.

The art director for *Duck Soup* was Wiard Ihnen, working for Paramount's supervisory art director, Hans Dreier. Ihnen provided the Marx Brothers with an abundance of overscaled Art Deco spaces, which resemble giant playrooms in an attempt to make the mad dictators, spies, and society types that inhabit them look ridiculous. It is almost impossible not to look silly when you are sleeping on a barge situated on a pedestal and you slide down from your bedroom to a state ballroom on a fireman's pole, as Groucho does in his first scene.

The ballroom itself is part Viennese, with huge, vertical windows resembling those of the fin-de-siècle artist Koloman Moser, and part early Fascist, with stone eagles hovering above 20-foot-high doors and massive, unembellished white walls. There are snail-shaped pedestals 5 feet high, portal windows the size of a bathysphere, and a Japanese screen as big as a drive-in movie screen.

The mere presence of these humorous architectural details is enough to get the message across, but typically of the Marx Brothers, enough is never enough. There is the sublime ridiculousness of scenes such as Harpo's ride through the streets of Freedonia, dressed up as Paul Revere. The presidential palace may be Art Deco stylistically, but the rural neighborhoods of the rest of the country are first preindustrial (thatched cottages), then contemporary urban (brownstones), and finally Native American (adobe brick)—and all on the same street. Nor is the famous mirror scene free from decorative incongruities. Despite all evidence to the contrary, including our witnessing the mirror shattering and Groucho and Harpo circling around the space like a pair of Sumo wrestlers, the wall decoration in the background and the armchair in the foreground maintain their mirror images throughout the scene.

Duck Soup is full of conventional Art Deco sets, such as Mrs. Teasdale's country estate, with its dropped ceiling, streamlined rooms, Tamara de Lempicka oils, and plethora of table lamps, but this is why she ends up having oranges thrown at her at the end of the movie. With the Marx Brothers, conventional behavior is too much to bear.

FRED AND GINGER

Wiard Ihnen made a total mockery of modern decor in *Duck Soup*. A more subtle approach was that chosen by Van Nest Polglase for the films he designed for Fred Astaire and Ginger Rogers in the thirties. Variations of these "big white sets," found throughout the years in interior design, film design, and that more elusive place known as the national psyche, have made them perhaps the most universally admired and instantly recognizable sets in Hollywood history.

Van Nest Polglase was born in Brooklyn, New York, in 1898; his unique name is a result of his family's Cornish heritage. Like many of the great Hollywood art directors, he studied architecture as a young man and disliked it enough to leave school before he was twenty-one. He began his career at Paramount and went over to RKO when David O. Selznick signed him on in 1932, remaining the supervisory art director for RKO for eleven years, until alcoholism began to interfere with his work; *Citizen Kane* (1941) was the last major film he worked on for RKO.

While Polglase's visual style played a tremendous part in the ultimate look of the Astaire/Rogers musicals, credit for the art direction of the majority of these films must go to the unit art director, Carroll Clark, and set decorator, Darrell Silvera. Clark would go on to become

Flying Down To Rio

Fred Astaire and Ginger Rogers have their first dance, the carioca. Glimpsed among the outrageous butterfly motif and the exotic costumes: Van Nest Polglase's and Carroll Clark's trademark pristine whites and jet blacks. (RKO)

RIGHT: *Top Hat* (1935)

This anonymous sketch from the RKO art department captures the shimmering elegance and stylishness that characterize the sets for every Fred Astaire musical. (RKO)

ABOVE: *Top Hat*

The world is a nightclub: the cast of Top Hat
performs "The Piccolino." (RKO)

RIGHT: *Top Hat*

Ersatz Venice. (RKO)

one of the great color art directors in history, ending his career with the magnificent *Mary Poppins* (1965), but special notice should be made of Silvera's often-unnoticed contributions. The credit for the set decorator is usually in such small print on the screen that few can read it even if they've bothered to stay in their seats that long, but in fact the set decorator can have as much control over what appears in front of the camera as the supervisor, since it is he who often chooses the style of telephone to sit on the night table or the kind of mirror to go on a wall. Set decorators often must cope with very large staffs—Silvera at one point supervised over one hundred people—and work on several films simultaneously. There are over three hundred films from 1932 until 1980 for which Silvera was the chief set decorator. (MGM's chief set decorator, Edwin B. Willis, has credits that run to nearly four hundred films.)

The first film to star Astaire and Rogers, with art direction by Polglase and Clark, was *Flying Down to Rio* (1933). Actually, Astaire and Rogers have peripheral roles, playing members of a touring band who get mixed up in an intercontinental romance between the actual stars of the film, Dolores Del Rio and Gene Raymond. Much of the film's jet-setting atmosphere—including its title—was predetermined by the interest of RKO producer Merian C. Cooper in aviation. Sikorsky and Pan American, two of the newest and biggest players in the industry, are featured prominently in *Flying Down to Rio,* as are radiograms, which were the heart of RKO's business ties with the RCA corporation.

Polglase's and Clark's addiction to big, white spaces and parallel lines is demonstrated even before Astaire takes a step. In the scene in the kitchen of the Hotel Hibiscus with which the film opens, the achingly white, sanitized, and sleek walls of the kitchen are juxtaposed against the stark, black tuxedos of the service staff. Later we get a glimpse of the hotel's Moorish ballroom. But nothing much electric happens until the cast and crew head for Rio de Janeiro, the Carioca Casino, and Fred and Ginger's first dance.

"The Carioca"—at eighteen minutes—is probably the longest single dance number in movie musical history, and Clark and his crew pull out all the stops to make it a visually memorable one. The casino is a white showcase, with a white staircase built out of stylized iron "vines" leading to a white balcony, surrounding a bandstand on which the members of the orchestra are wearing white sombreros. Here, as in other Astaire/Rogers musicals, the art direction creates such extreme contrasts of white and black as to dissolve the illusion of depth, turning the dancing figures, the floor, and the scenic background into flat, graphic shapes that in turn emphasize the two-dimensional nature of the film image. It is an effect at once disconcerting, because the image on the screen shifts in its reality, and exhilarating, because it is so visually dazzling. Those used to watching—or unfortunately forced to watch—this scene on a tiny video screen can only imagine the sensation it must have caused at a scale of 25 feet.

Much more dazzling, because it contains more Astaire and Rogers and shows more confidence in its visual style, is the fourth picture Astaire and Rogers and Polglase and Clark made together—*Top Hat* (1935). For one thing, *Top Hat*'s director, Mark Sandrich, was more talented and experienced than *Rio*'s Thornton Freeland. For another, the score by Irving Berlin was longer and more memorable. (Vincent Youmans contributed *Rio*'s three songs.) Lastly, the effervescent sense of humor and parody to be found in the settings is featured more prominently here.

In *Top Hat,* Astaire is a Broadway star engaged by a London producer (played by Edward Everett Horton, the Margaret Dumont of Astaire films), and Rogers is the kept society woman he meets and loves. The plot of mistaken identities is unimportant; what is important are the songs and dances.

The numerous sets employed for *Top Hat*'s musical numbers are all, of course, white, from the hotel room in which Astaire performs "No Strings," to the bandstand where he courts Rogers in the rain to "Isn't This a Lovely Day?" to the Venetian-style nightclub of "Cheek to Cheek." In a world increasingly ravished by poverty and impending war, Polglase's predilection for chromatic virginity was reassuring: the walls, awnings, divans, bureaus, statues, columns, sconces, as well as the bow ties, gowns, and occasionally hats and shoes are all blindingly white.

At times the whiteness and gigantism of the sets are implausible to the point of satire, proving that it was still okay to laugh at modern architecture and the playgrounds of the rich. The hotel room in London that Astaire and Horton inhabit in the first half of the movie is larger than a penthouse, and the set in Venice—part canal, part airport, as well as pieces of a restaurant, a nightclub, and Saint Mark's Square—is overrun by Moorish towers, Renaissance oculi, and twisted columns, trestles, and moldings. These sets are classic examples of how Hollywood can take a genuine artistic movement and translate it into something inauthentic but popular—the Art Deco sets in London and the Orientalism of Venice are exaggerations of architectural trends of the twenties. In London we see RKO's idea of the streamlined functionalism of architects like Walter Gropius and designers like Gerrit Rietveld, who promoted simplicity and geometry in their work, while Venice is pure fantasy, a conflation of current design trends with late-Victorian Art Nouveau.

The work of Polglase and Clark pays off particularly well in two scenes in *Top Hat*—both dance numbers, as to be expected. In the first example, Astaire and Rogers meet in a music pavilion in a deserted corner of what is supposed to be Hyde Park. It is raining, and Rogers (who has been riding) is forced to dismount and take cover. Astaire has been following her, and he courts her with a song and dance, "Isn't This a Lovely Day?"

As Astaire sings, then dances, then coaxes an initially reluctant Rogers into joining him, the music pavilion changes very subtly from prop to participant. The pavilion frame is white, of course—a bud-and-flower wrought-iron pattern that is more Art Nouveau than Art Deco. In the pavilion proper, there are alternating white benches and ornate music stands (also white, apparently iron as well). The pavilion frame, benches, and music stands create triangles and rectangles above and around the dancers, making a visual counterpoint to the melody and the dancing. By the use of this architectural detail, director Sandrich and designers Polglase and Clark have put quotation marks around the performance of Astaire and Rogers, lifting it out of the film by stressing its cinematic qualities, those qualities that flatten the film surface and give all the Astaire/Rogers numbers their amazing graphic effect.

The second payoff comes in the Venetian half of the movie. The charade of mistaken identities has progressed to a crisis: Rogers is being encouraged by her best friend's wife to dance with a man (Astaire) who she thinks is her friend's husband. This takes place in the ersatz nightclub that Polglase and Clark have represented as being in Venice. The Venice of the studio, however, has little in common with the actual Queen of the Adriatic (except water on the set). It is a Disneyland Lido where supposedly grown-up people waltz about (literally) in yard-wide hats while sitting under white, mushroom-shaped lampshades in a dining room that resembles the prow of an ocean liner.

Astaire and Rogers are on a crowded dance floor the size of a football field; he is singing "Cheek to Cheek." All of a sudden, in one glorious camera pan, the lyrics break off, the music swells, and Astaire dances his partner across a footbridge and onto a terrace. The crowd is gone—there is nothing but the two dancers and one pristine white Renaissance doorway with a trellis, enclosed by a rusticated white horseshoe-shaped wall. Again, the set frames the dancers. This time, however, their dance is less athletic, more romantic, as if to emphasize their impending union. To echo this, the set is sheltering and enclosed. The overture in the pavilion in the rain is resolved in the reprise on the terrace. Although the props serve a similar function, they contribute different meanings. The doorway and arch promise balance and resolution, whereas the pavilion in the park was only a momentary diversion out of the rain. This promise is kept when, at the end of the dance, the door opens and Astaire and Rogers pass through it together.

Top Hat concludes with "The Piccolino," a bit of triumphant foolishness that pushes the production right over the cliff of believability (where, granted, it had been hovering all along). Supposedly, Carnival has begun in Venice and the natives and visitors are no longer able to restrain their desire to sing, dance, and show off the entire RKO wardrobe. Two adjoining sound stages were pressed into service for this number, and a canal was built through them with the water dyed black to make the set appear even whiter. It's a good excuse for several long shots of the ultimate big white set.

CITIZEN KANE

By 1940, with Europe at war and the United States very close to war, the American public was no longer in the mood for carefree satire. Far from accepting the utopian notions suggested by modern architecture, with its democratic spaces and strict functionalism, the nation instead turned to its past. In the late thirties there was a pronounced increase in the popularity of early Americana, evidenced, for example, by the restoration of Colonial Williamsburg. The past was something to be treasured and preserved, the future feared and mistrusted.

Most of the studios regeared their efforts for the new job of inspiring confidence and signaling danger. Gone were the flippant treatments of playboys and chorus girls amid pleasure palaces. At Paramount, Hans Dreier was already making the switch from elegance to decadence, from the salacious *The Devil Is a Woman* (1935) to the early noir tension of *The Glass Key* (1942). Anton Grot at Warner Brothers and Cedric Gibbons at MGM followed a similar tack. And at RKO, Van Nest Polglase supervised the art direction of what is considered by many to be the best film ever made in America, *Citizen Kane* (1941).

But it would be wrong to grant Polglase anything more than cursory credit for the art direction in *Citizen Kane;* by this time his problems with alcohol and his inability to deal with the changing artistic and financial climate in the industry had forced him to the fringe. The real art director of *Citizen Kane* was its unit art director, Perry Ferguson, one of the truly deserving unsung heroes of Hollywood art direction. He had a long, stellar career with RKO, beginning as a sketch artist and mov-

Citizen Kane (1941)

Art director Perry Ferguson's keynote throughout the film: reversal of scale, as Kane (Orson Welles) finds himself dwarfed by the illusion he has created. (RKO)

ing up to comedies like *Bringing Up Baby* (1938). After *Citizen Kane,* he worked for Samuel Goldwyn on *The Best Years of Our Lives* (1946) and for Warner Brothers on *Rope* (1948). Ferguson frequently labored without proper credit, and his contributions have been largely unrecorded for posterity. Pauline Kael's *The Citizen Kane Book* doesn't even mention him (or Polglase either, for that matter). Most scholarly studies of the film talk at length about its creator, Orson Welles, or its cinematographer, Gregg Toland, and the screenplay, credited to Welles and Herman J. Mankiewicz.

One of the little-known facts about *Citizen Kane* is

LEFT: *Citizen Kane*

The completed hall, while similar to the sketch in scale, is much less ornate, due to RKO's severe budget problems. (RKO)

BELOW: *Citizen Kane*

One of Claude Gillingwater, Jr.'s evocative sketches for the great hall of Xanadu. (RKO)

Citizen Kane

Kane (Orson Welles) addresses the staff of the Inquirer. *(RKO)*

how inexpensive it was to produce. Welles was a newcomer to Hollywood—a twenty-five-year-old kid—and RKO, even if it was solvent, which it wasn't, budgeted only for what was absolutely necessary. Ferguson and Toland were more in the nature of spies, requested by Welles and acceded to by RKO primarily with the provision that they keep Welles on a financial leash. They were practically the only RKO employees on the set, for Welles recruited his entire cast and a great deal of his technical support from the Mercury Theater company he ran back East.

Ferguson was trained as a set constructor, not an illustrator, so he and Welles hired a team of sketch artists, including Claude Gillingwater, Jr., and ransacked research libraries full of historical designs for their ideas. Apparently Polglase was out of the loop entirely—Ferguson reported directly to Welles and needed only Welles's permission to begin blueprinting and constructing sets.

As originally designed, *Citizen Kane* was to have several sets that were among the largest ever built. Welles's model for Xanadu, Kane's mansion, was less

William Randolph Hearst's San Simeon than D. W. Griffith's Babylon and Cecil B. DeMille's Egypt. But the budget department at RKO would hear none of it, so several changes had to be made between the planning stage and the execution. Whole sets were canceled: a scene in a living room in Xanadu with Kane (played by Orson Welles) and Susan Alexander (Dorothy Comingore) was moved to the Great Hall. Pieces of property from Darrell Silvera's vaults were wheeled out to fill up the spaces. This is probably what accounts for the perfectly in-character juxtaposition of every style of art in the room—Art Deco, Egyptian, Victorian, English Gothic, French Regency, and Spanish Baroque.

The entire mood of the film was altered substantially by one cost-cutting maneuver that Ferguson dreamed up to appease Toland's need for deep spaces. Bare parts of the sets were draped with huge rolls of black velvet that, when photographed, appear to lead the space on the screen into infinity. Thus rooms that merely consisted of a white plaster balustrade, a candelabra, and a staircase when combined with the proper perspective produced the illusion of traveling hundreds of feet into the background. Not only did this save money, it also increased the mysterious aura surrounding Kane and his life and gave the film a brooding and fragmented look that increased its efficacy. Additionally, the sets could be only partly lit, saving electricity as well.

There are many scenes in the film where Ferguson's sets are framed against Kane's personality or seen as symbols in relation to Kane's life. In the sequence where Mr. Thatcher is taking young Charles away to school, the boy is framed by a window in the rooming house his mother runs. When his father gets up to close the window against the cold, his mother gets up to open it again. The window of opportunity is most metaphorically displayed. The low ceilings of the *Inquirer* office are also unable to contain Kane's ambition, as Toland continually photographs Welles with the dark, beamed ceiling pushing down upon his head. When Kane finally gets a building scaled to the size he has always demanded—Xanadu—it swallows him up.

The famous rally scene includes a monumental poster of Kane's head, which is the only part of Kane that is scaled properly to the size of the hall, supposedly Madison Square Garden, but more resembling a Roman amphitheater or a Nazi rally. The man Kane is but a slen-

Citizen Kane

The symbolic use of disorganized space: an enraged and defeated Kane (Orson Welles) rages after Jim Gettys (Ray Collins). (RKO)

Citizen Kane

Another example of Perry Ferguson's use of reversal of scale: Kane (Orson Welles) contemplates the distance—socially as well as physically—between him and his wife, Susan Alexander (Dorothy Comingore). (RKO)

der dot when compared with the illusion of him hanging down from the rafters. Again Ferguson's set expresses something about the man that the screenplay and the actor cannot.

In the end, Ferguson's art direction for *Citizen Kane* constitutes a musing on the architectural nature of power. Gone is the playfulness of incompetent dictators like Groucho Marx's Rufus T. Firefly, with his bargelike bed and overscaled toy palace; gone, too, are the clean, well-lighted dance floors of white purity that RKO created for Fred and Ginger just eight years earlier. People who build buildings are powerful, and people who are

powerful are dangerous. At the rally in Madison Square Garden or smashing Susan's bedroom at Xanadu, Kane has turned into a powerful monster, and the selfishness of his power makes the spaces he built seem sinister and unsettling.

Ferguson's fragmented sets equal Kane's fragmented life. The pieces of the jigsaw puzzle Susan works on in Xanadu to alleviate her boredom are symbols of the pieces of the puzzle that add up to Kane's story, as are his fragmented reflections in a hall mirror or a glass snowball. In the end, and in every sense of the word, "Rosebud" is only a prop.

BRAZIL

Citizen Kane hinted at the danger that lurks in a society that trusts an image more than it trusts reality; *Brazil* (1985) shows us the inevitable result. *Brazil* is the story of a country where no one means what they say, nothing looks like what it is, and no one notices.

Directed with macabre flair by Monty Python member Terry Gilliam, *Brazil* is, on the surface, the dramatic story of one man, Sam Lowry (Jonathan Pryce), and his crusade against a totalitarian society that spies on all its citizens, subverts them into being automatons, and mesmerizes them with posters, television, and especially old movies. In fact, almost everyone—including Sam until his conscience is awakened—behaves as if they are in an old movie, dressing in forties fashions, talking about their looks and their lovers, and decorating their "homes" with pieces of popular culture. Even the title song comes straight from the forties.

Set "somewhere in the twentieth century," *Brazil*'s production design is neither nostalgic nor futuristic, but both, usually simultaneously. Office workers watch *Casablanca* (1942) on tiny television screens inserted into their video-display terminals, which in turn are mounted atop old manual typewriters. An apartment—with shag rugs on the floor, petal-leaf table lamps, and a bathtub with feet—is pierced by thick, snakelike ventilation/surveillance ducts. Diners in the most elegant restaurants get globs of blue mush on their plates with a beautiful color photograph of what they are actually eating inserted in a menu card before them. Machines that perform incredibly modern tasks are cased in antiquated, streamlined packages, making them belong neither to the forties nor to the eighties.

The amazing sets for *Brazil* were designed by Norman Garwood, one of the preeminent production designers working today. (He was nominated for an Academy Award for *Brazil* and again for *Glory* in 1989.) Every scene in *Brazil* is loaded with displacement and terror due to the illogic of the design. The housing block that Sam lives in appears to be a monolithic cube of several dozen stories, definitely an apparition from the future, yet the offices of the Ministry of Information where he works resemble an old printing-press room in a newspaper factory, with frosted-glass partitions and an elevator with an old-fashioned metal accordion gate. Sam's mother visits a plastic surgeon whose office is set inside what looks like a deconsecrated Russian Orthodox church.

Garwood's settings emphasize the inhumanity of the characters' lives by depriving them of every unpleasant aspect of human existence. They don't have to work hard, never grow old, and can buy anything they want, provided they fill out all the forms properly and question no one's authority. In fact, it is a mistake on a form, caused literally by a bug in a computer, that instigates the Rube Goldbergian plot that eventually sucks Sam into the bowels of the society (and they do appear to be bowels—the tubes, wires, and ducts that provide all these wonders for the citizens seem to breathe and bleed and sometimes even excrete like humans).

Along the way, Garwood borrows heavily from other movies to show how a society addicted to illusions can only become an illusion itself. There is the very Chaplinesque scene between Sam and his adjacent worker, fighting over the one desk that has been partitioned between their two minuscule metal cubes. There is a reference to *Metropolis* (1926) in Sam's dream of going to battle against a metal robot, and to *Potemkin* (1925) and its plunging baby carriage. There are old movie sets, like Sam's mother's apartment, via Gloria Swanson in *Sunset Boulevard* (1950). Bernardo Bertolucci's *The Conformist* (1970) shows up in the scenes with faceless bureaucrats behind tiny desks set in huge, blank, echo-filled rooms. And there are the old movies themselves—the Marx Brothers and *Casablanca*—that the entire city seems to watch around the clock.

Brazil is unmistakably a masterpiece of postmodern film design; it trashes architectural and design history and reassembles it to fit its own iconoclastic tastes, much the way contemporary architecture and design stick a Greek temple inside a mall or an Indian headdress on top of a Regency mantelpiece. The world, thanks to television and movies, is too much with us. The great, good nature with which Hollywood greeted modern architecture in the twenties and early thirties quickly gave way to skepticism. *Brazil* is evidence that this skepticism has unmistakably evolved into downright terror. The vision of the world that Gilliam and Garwood present in *Brazil* is not that of the distant future, which we can try to avoid, nor that of the recent past, from which we can learn. It is, unfortunately, the present, and there is nowhere else to hide.

A STRANGER WORLD: THE ART OF SCIENCE FICTION

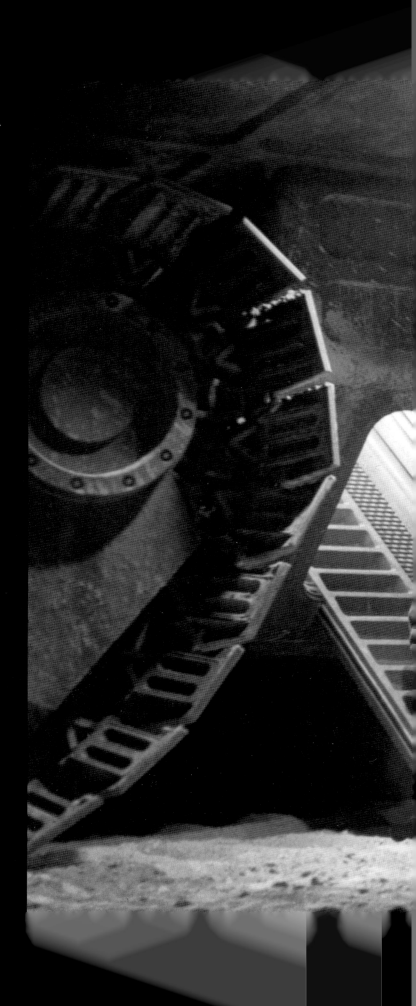

The ability of the movie camera to make magic has always attracted filmmakers to science fiction. One of the first films ever produced, Georges Méliès's *A Trip to the Moon* (1902), established space travel and creatures from the beyond as the twin anchors of the genre. Science fiction has grown more popular over the years only as its audience has become more sophisticated and technology has advanced. The depiction of the world of the future depends on cinematic trickery more than does any other genre. Thus, any discussion of the history of art direction in the science-fiction film must take into account the accomplishments of the special-effects department, which shares the spotlight in science fiction with the art director and the production designer.

The basic components of special effects are the glass shot, rear projection, matte paintings, and miniature models. Although computer animation has replaced many formerly complicated effects, process shots still possess a certain grace and finesse that no machine can properly duplicate. They are still used when a particularly vivid and purely cinematic effect is needed.

A glass shot is prepared by having members of the art department paint the wings or background of a scene onto a

Star Wars (1977) *The Jawas in front of their land tank. (Fox)*

Vincent Korda's incredible set for Everytown (read London), c. 1940. With William Cameron Menzies directing, it is easy to see why this is one of the most impressively designed films in history. (United Artists)

Everytown convincingly in ruins (United Artists)

clear pane of glass, which is then set up midway between the camera and the constructed set. In the finished picture, the painted scene will complement the real image. For instance, the Alps might be painted behind a studio cottage, transporting the setting from the Hollywood hills to Switzerland. With rear projection, film is played behind an actor, who is lit in such a manner that no shadows appear. When filmed, the actor appears to be in the scene behind him. The art department is also involved with matte paintings and miniature models. In the former, a painted scene is pinned to the wall of the studio and the part of the scene where the live action is to occur is blacked out. Later, the film laboratory will superimpose the live action over the blacked-out portion of the matte and the entire scene will appear complete. Miniatures are often far from small; they can be anywhere from one to hundreds of feet long, but they are still cheaper than constructing an entire building to scale and are particularly useful for rocket ships landing on the earth or hurtling through space.

THINGS TO COME

Although Hollywood produced a few successful science-fiction films throughout the twenties and thirties, such as *Just Imagine* (1930) and the *Flash Gordon* serials, the first masterpiece of Hollywood art direction in science fiction was a British production, *Things to Come* (1936).

Things to Come was directed by William Cameron Menzies, who had already established himself in the United States as one of the most ambitious art directors of his era. The sets were designed by Vincent Korda, brother of the film's producer, Alexander Korda, and the special effects were designed by the great Ned Mann, who began his career working for Menzies twelve years earlier on *The Thief of Bagdad* (1924). (Mann would continue Menzies's heritage, training the next generation of special-effects designers, including Wally Veevers, who worked on *2001: A Space Odyssey.*)

With such a rich pool of talent, plus the active par-

TOP: *Things to Come*

The film begins to date when the "space gun" is built and the citizens of Everytown begin to riot. Throughout the silliness, Vincent Korda never lost his sense of streamlined design. (United Artists)

ABOVE: *Things to Come*

Is it an earth-moving machine or an overgrown vacuum cleaner? In reality, it's a miniature model, barely 4 feet long. (United Artists)

OPPOSITE: *Things to Come*

Everytown, 2036. Not a hotel atrium but the public square of the city of the future. (United Artists)

ticipation of H. G. Wells, who wrote the original book and collaborated on the screenplay, it was inevitable that *Things to Come* would be magnificent in its virtues—and equally magnificent in its flaws. Its virtues, primarily, are the astounding visual effects, convincing, despite their datedness, due to the sheer inventiveness of Menzies, Korda, and Mann. Its flaws are mostly the responsibility of Wells, who saddled the movie with a speech-filled screenplay that barely allows the actors to address each other, and somewhat of Menzies, who was inexperienced as a director.

Vincent Korda began his career somewhat reluctantly, but blossomed into one of the most diversified production designers in film history, equally at home in every genre. Trained as a painter, Korda was working in the south of France when his brother, upset with the visual direction his production of *Marius* (1931) was taking, and knowing full well Vincent's love of the French landscape, asked Vincent to go to Marseilles and prepare some sketches for him that might be utilized for the sets. Before long, Vincent was in Paris supervising the construction of the sets he had sketched, and the rest is history. Most notable among Vincent Korda's many credits are the remake of *The Thief of Bagdad* (1940), the wonderful historicism of *That Hamilton Woman* (1941), the mesmerizing postwar Vienna of *The Third Man* (1950), and Venice, in all its glory, in *Summertime* (1955).

Alexander Korda was by all accounts a kind and generous, if sometimes overbearing, man, and he tried to do right by everyone involved in the production of *Things to Come.* He bent over backward to accommodate the irascible Wells (at one point, Wells criticized Arthur Bliss's beautiful score with the offhand comment that "the machines of the future will make no noise") and offered fellow Hungarian expatriate László Moholy-Nagy a chance to design some of the sets (though his designs, for whatever reason, were never used). He also gave the production a lot of money—$1.5 million, his most expensive picture to date.

It shows. The opening sequence, the destruction of London (called Everytown in the film) at Christmas 1940, is one of the most emotionally disturbing and realistic depictions of a bombing raid on a major city ever produced. The heart-tugging shots of the filtering snow and the children selecting sweets become a nightmare of

The War of the Worlds (1953)

The greatest flying saucer ever designed—Albert Nozaki's streamlined Martian hovercraft, a predatory, cyclopean boomerang. (Paramount)

crumbling bricks and anonymous citizens turned into clones behind their gas masks. Vincent Korda's admiration for the techniques of German Expressionism show in his choice of darkly lit streets and distorted angles. As a slight bit of black humor, the first building to be destroyed by the enemy's bombs is a cinema.

The second half of the movie, set in 2036, takes place in the giant underworld city of Everytown, where the glass-tube elevators, stacked curvilinear balconies, and clear plastic lounge chairs resemble nothing so much as the atrium of a Hyatt Hotel or the lobby of an international airport. This comes after a sequence depicting the construction of the city with huge hydraulic and electric machines (actually miniatures), which do not look at all futuristic, and uncannily presages the visual style of Pare Lorentz's Depression-era documentaries *The Plow That Broke the Plains* (1936) and *The River* (1937). By the time we get to the "space gun" (which looks like a giant electric tooth-

brush) and Raymond Massey as Oswald Cabal making his final speech about "all the universe or nothing-ness . . . which shall it be?" *Things to Come* has proven itself to be a dazzling, dated masterpiece.

KEEP WATCHING THE SKIES

More datedness comes in the form of the "alien invasion" films of the fifties. The Communist peril lurked behind the message of nearly every film of that decade, in the form of strange neighbors, organized crime, or outright military takeovers, but never more symbolically, or with more visual verve than in science fiction. Nearly five hundred science-fiction films were made by the major studios and independents in the years 1950 to 1962, more than at any other time in film history. Many of these, of course, were produced for teenagers, as they continue to be, and the vast majority aren't worth seeing twice. But a few can rightly claim to be masterpieces, and through the magnificence of their art direction they have left an indelible visual memory on the consciousness of the filmgoing public.

First among them is *The War of the Worlds* (1953). Again based on a book by H. G. Wells, this time updated to contemporary California, *The War of the Worlds* was directed by a former editor, Byron Haskin, and produced by one of the masters of 1950s science fiction, George Pal (*When Worlds Collide,* 1951, and *The Time Machine,* 1960). The art direction was by Albert Nozaki, working with Hal Pereira, then Paramount's supervisory art director, and the special effects were produced by six people, including Gordon Jennings, whose contributions to film history are particularly noteworthy.

Although a cliché, it is fair to say that cinema truly is a collaborative art, and a discussion of the merits of the art direction of *The War of the Worlds* without mention of its special-effects supervisor would be a great injustice. Jennings was the head of Paramount's special-effects department from 1935 until his death in 1953. He worked most often for Cecil B. DeMille, perfecting several effects processes such as moving titles and the split screen. He won many Academy Awards; his last, for *The War of the Worlds,* was—sadly—posthumous.

The art direction and special effects of *The War of the Worlds* are deceptively straightforward and simple: once an effect is shown for the first time for dramatic purposes, it is merely repeated in an ever-accelerating tempo until some sort of resolution occurs and the story moves on. For instance, the first appearance of the incinerating ray, killing the three men who are guarding the crash site, is a shocking blend of burning welding wire, stage smoke, and high-pitched electric sounds, but the effect doesn't get any worse, only much more frequent as the film progresses. We accept the ray and the damage it does, and thus are entirely convinced it is real.

Likewise, Nozaki's settings for the film are created entirely to reassure us, which makes it that much more devastating when they are so utterly destroyed. Before the Martians arrive on the scene, we are witness to a square dance at the local social hall, where the hero, Dr. Clayton Forrester (Gene Barry), and the minister's niece, Sylvia van Buren (Ann Robinson), first get acquainted. The wooden barn walls swelling with the sound of the sweet music and the kids drinking soda pop

TOP: *The War of the Worlds*

An unused design for the Martians. (Paramount)

ABOVE:

Alexander Golitzen (right) in 1945, later to be Universal's supervisory art director, showing sketches to producer Walter Wanger.

are symbols of the simple peace in which we hope to live our lives and which the evil, world-conquering aliens wish to destroy.

This trope (which is almost entirely absent from Wells's novel) occurs over and over again throughout *The War of the Worlds.* Sylvia and Dr. Forrester take refuge against the invasion first in a farmhouse, where they have a chance to enjoy a hearty breakfast of bacon and fried eggs before the house is flattened by a saucer. Later, they take cover in a church, a loaded symbol if ever there was one. The Martians succeed in smashing the church's stained-glass window but they have no defense against prayer, nor against, as Cedric Hardwicke explains at the conclusion, "the littlest things, which God in His wisdom had put on this earth." He is referring to microbes, but he might as well have meant us.

The most famous of Nozaki's creations for *The War of the Worlds* are the spacecraft and its inhabitants. The hovercraft—basically an upturned saucer with an antenna on top, like a streamlined Hoover vacuum cleaner—is probably the most famous spaceship model in movie history. It is what a flying saucer should look like, and it appears to be wholly practical. The saucers were originally held up by electronic beams, which, however, threatened to burn down the set and were replaced by guide wires. The Martians themselves make only fleeting appearances, most notably in the farmhouse scene, when one pink and pruny creature scuttles by an open window. The monster was personally designed by Nozaki and Charles Gemora, and Gemora had the double honor of actually wearing the costume on camera.

Another great scene, parallel in its epic scope and sense of realism to the opening scenes of *Things to Come,* is the evacuation and destruction of Los Angeles. By combining documentarylike footage of cars plodding slowly along on flat tires and refugees lining the free-

ways with shots of miniature buildings being blasted by Martian heat rays, Nozaki and Pereira create a true aura of utter hopelessness inside the city limits. The scene culminates in the classic shot of Gene Barry, clothes torn and dirty, running alone through the abandoned, shelled corridors of the once-great city, searching for Sylvia while rows of spacecrafts fire heat rays above his head. In the end the world is saved, but not before we see a shot of a Martian hand, pitifully anemic, squiggling out of the doomed machine and falling dead and limp, one last wave from one of the greatest effects masters—Gordon Jennings—on his last film.

A similar message, though not nearly as grave, is to be found in *This Island Earth* (1955), produced by William Alland (the reporter in *Citizen Kane*) and directed by Joseph Newman with evident assistance from Jack Arnold (*The Creature from the Black Lagoon,* 1954). The art direction was supervised by the great Alexander Golitzen (most famous for his work with Alfred Hitchcock and Max Ophüls), with unit direction by Richard H. Riedel. Riedel's forte was fantastic detail, an impossible building here or an outrageous prop there, which—though patently improbable—gives his films a certain playfulness and enlivens them visually. Examples of this abound in *This Island Earth,* from the "interociter," which resembles a black jukebox, to the famous mutant alien, with his bug eyes and exposed cranium.

This Island Earth tells the story of Cal Meachem (Rex Reason), a crack pilot and nuclear scientist, and his recruitment by leaders of the planet Metaluna, ostensibly to help save them from alien destruction (of course, they're secretly plotting to alter our minds and take over the earth). Cal is aided by a former girlfriend, Ruth Adams (Faith Domergue), and challenged by a Metalunian leader, Exeter (Jeff Morrow).

The high point of this lunacy, visually, is Metaluna itself. The surface of the planet is pocked with craters, and its inhabitants are forced to live below the surface in towering buildings with Saturn-like rings and clear glass domes, some shaped amorphously to resemble paintings by Salvador Dali. Much of this work was done with a 110-foot-long model of the planet, with a few matte paintings for the most epic effects. The film's most dramatic sequence comes nearly at the end, when one of the mutant creatures manages to scramble aboard the escaping spaceship and attacks Ruth while she, Cal, and

OPPOSITE, ABOVE:
This Island Earth (1955)

A preliminary sketch for the fantastic surface of the planet Metaluna. (Universal)

OPPOSITE, BELOW:
This Island Earth

A pastel drawing of a rocket design. (Universal)

This Island Earth

Special effects in action: preparing a process shot of a full-scale matte. (Universal)

INSET: *This Island Earth*

As a shelf of mute busts look on, a Universal technician proudly displays full-size and miniature mutant alien models. (Universal)

OPPOSITE:
This Island Earth

It's hard to make a flying saucer stand still for its picture. (Universal)

Exeter are stuck inside the "conversion tubes," which supposedly readjust their body masses for earth's atmosphere. The effects are standard, but the mutant—a rejected design from *It Came from Outer Space* (1953)—is a classic.

More importantly, *This Island Earth* began to point the way to the future of science-fiction films, away from the visions of mass destruction and a faceless, emotionless society (read Communism) toward scenes of interplanetary cooperation, the spiritual quest of space travel, and the increased dominance of special effects. At least for science fiction, the era of the single art director, in control of the entire production and responsible for the look of the completed picture, was over.

2001: A SPACE ODYSSEY

By any standard, *2001: A Space Odyssey* (1968) is one of the most important science-fiction films ever made. It rendered all previous attempts at showing interplanetary travel obsolete, and the structure and technique of its special effects resonated throughout the industry for nearly ten years. *2001* is also unique among science-fiction films in its lack of a fixed image of the future. While most films of this genre feel the need to latch onto a specific time frame, more or less a vision of the earth transformed, *2001* refers to the distant past and the unimaginable future, somewhere on earth and somewhere beyond the stars, with the central section set in the year 2001 functioning merely as a bridge between the two "worlds."

2001: A Space Odyssey was written, directed, and partially designed by Stanley Kubrick. Also involved in the production design were Tony Masters, Harry Lange (a former NASA engineer), and Ernest Archer, with additional special photographic effects by the venerable Wally Veevers, Douglas Trumbull, Con Pederson, and

Tom Howard. Already we can see how *2001* brought production design to a new level—for all practical purposes there are eight art directors at work. Unique, too, was the way in which Kubrick and his crew hired product designers to create the world of the future: McDonnell-Douglas helped plan the spaceships, IBM the computers, RCA the communications devices, and even Parker Brothers worked on the pens.

The film is divided into three segments: "The Dawn of Man," set on earth many millions of years ago; the middle, narrative segment, set on the moon and in the *Discovery* spaceship on the way to Jupiter; and "Jupiter and beyond the Infinite," which ends the film with a variety of extraordinary special effects. Kubrick, Masters, and the others invented several new techniques for use in *2001*. Front projection, which uses a two-way mirror to superimpose live action on top of a prefilmed background and is decidedly more credible than rear projection, was used for the first time in a major motion picture for the scenes of Africa and the desert in "The Dawn of Man," and Trumbull's "slit-scan" device, which manipulates the light coming into the camera, forms the basis of the entire "Star Gate" sequence near the end of the film.

2001: A Space Odyssey (1968)

The Hilton Space Station. (MGM)

Many of the design elements of the middle, narrative portion of the film now seem to be reflections of swinging London circa 1968 rather than the imagined near future. The stewardesses' uniforms, designed by Hardy Amies, look like the uncomfortable unisex pant suits that were being foisted on the innocent public in the late sixties, though they are still a great improvement over Raymond Massey's toga in *Things to Come.* The chairs in the space station lounge, created by Olivier Mourgue, are decidedly "mod" and would probably embarrass any twenty-first–century designer. But other innovations are in turn humorous, prescient, or unnerving, such as the "zero-gravity toilet," the videotape monitors, or HAL, the "perfect" computer who goes totally insane.

Kubrick and his company took great care to make the scenes in the middle section of the film scientifically accurate. Views of the earth, the moon, and the planets seen through the windows of the various spacecrafts throughout the film were calibrated to exactly imitate reality, down to the speed of their orbits. The interior of the *Discovery* on its way to Jupiter was a fully functioning centrifuge, weighing 38 tons. The unit was sealed during filming, and Kubrick directed the movements of the actors and the hidden cameras via radio and television monitors.

One of the great joys of *2001: A Space Odyssey* is the way in which Kubrick and Masters delight in constantly inverting and reinventing science-fiction clichés. The old standby spaceship, more or less a space jet, here looks like a wrench set with a bathysphere stuck to the end of it, or like two pieces of wheel-shaped pasta stuck together like dumbbells. Geometric shapes, primarily circles and rectangles, go beyond mere design principles and become symbols: the circular shape of the space "pods," HAL's "eye," the *Discovery* centrifuge, and close-ups of David Bowman's eyes reflect the cyclical nature of the film, which begins with "The Dawn of Man" and ends with the impending birth of the Star Child. The rectangle, in the form of the monolithic black slab that bedevils every creature in all sections of the movie, is the opposing force that prevents the circle from ever closing, most literally expressed in a shot at the very beginning of the "Beyond the Infinite" section, where the slab is aligned with the sun and several small planets as if it, too, was part of the natural order of the universe. It also should be noted that the entire second half of the middle sec-

tion, in which the *Discovery* sails toward Jupiter, is in reality one set, constantly explored by Kubrick's camera in ways that distort it through his use of concave and convex lenses (in themselves parts of circles), and that the concluding section involves no set construction at all, save for two eerily designed, pseudo-eighteenth-century rooms.

This concluding segment, with David Bowman (Keir Dullea) in his space suit watching what appears to be a much older version of himself eating dinner (real food, not space slush) and then dying in bed, is puzzling but admittedly less strange than it first seemed in more innocent times. The incongruity of our lives has caught up to us. A room that looked like a Baroque fantasy in 1968 now more closely resembles a tony hotel room decorated in somewhat poor taste. Strauss comes up on the soundtrack, the Star Child takes his place among the heavenly bodies, and the film concludes. In its audacity, in its ability to challenge the viewer with new ideas and to couch them in an appealing, if enigmatic, visual design, *2001: A Space Odyssey* remains unsurpassed.

RETRO SCI-FI

In the seventies and eighties the tempo of the times increased exponentially: life became even more fragmented, illogical, and distant. The gap between rich and poor and young and old seemed to grow greater even as television and other media brought us closer together. Hollywood—as it always had—mirrored these changes, offering pictures of a violent and moral-free society. Meanwhile, the studios broke up and budgets routinely climbed into the tens of millions and above. The invention and proliferation of video technology allowed all films to become instantly accessible, thus completely demystified.

One of Hollywood's responses to this demystification was to reinvent its own mythology. It discovered that the best place to go to rediscover its mythical connection to its audience was itself: the newest thing in science-fiction motion picture design is the past. Two films in particular exemplify this latest discovery of old Hollywood genres reborn as science fiction, George Lucas's *Star Wars* (1977) and Ridley Scott's *Blade Runner* (1982). Although the characters in *Star Wars* conduct interplanetary travel and live among aliens, the film is quite clearly set in the past—the prologue begins "a long time ago, in a galaxy far, far away. . . ." That past is not so far away, however, that it can't be reconstructed as a combination of old *Flash Gordon* serials (thus taking us full circle, back to the earliest science-fiction films) and war movies. *Blade Runner,* supposedly set in twenty-first-century Los Angeles, is nothing if not film noir with aliens, with star Harrison Ford as the Philip Marlowe of the interplanetary set.

Star Wars so quickly reached the level of classic status (it is still one of the largest grossing films in history) that its technical virtuosity and visual creativity are easily taken for granted. In retrospect, it can be seen that *Star Wars,* like *2001* before it, completely changed the audience's expectations for science fiction. But whereas *2001,* true to the tenor of its time, opted for expanding and challenging those expectations and thus paving the way for a futuristic model of the universe, *Star Wars* caters to the audience, turning the light of the future backward, to a lost world of courageous heroes and clear-cut enemies—a perfect world for the soon-to-come, greed-driven, Reagan-era America of the eighties.

The production designer for *Star Wars* was John Barry, with tremendous assistance from the now-fabled Los Angeles–based group Industrial Light and Magic, art directors Norman Reynolds and Leslie Dilley, and special photographic effects supervisor John Dykstra. One of the ways in which the production design crew evinced a cozy familiarity in the settings within the conventions of a science-fiction film was to use common objects and transform their function, thus making the audience's transference that much easier. Examples abound: the robots look like human beings (and R2D2 and C3PO are reminiscent of Laurel and Hardy), Luke Skywalker's home looks like a stone igloo (foreign, but not too foreign),

Star Wars

Designer Norman Reynolds made excellent use of the earth's natural wonders to suggest another galaxy "far, far away." (Fox)

and the garbage chute is a giant trash compactor.

At times, *Star Wars* more than suggests film history, it actually reproduces it. There is the scene with Luke (Mark Hamill) and Han Solo (Harrison Ford) in the firing pit of the *Millennium Falcon* on the final assault on the Death Star—lovingly lifted, shot-by-shot, from an old Hollywood aerial dogfight—or the final sequence at the rebel medal ceremony, which echoes *The Wizard of Oz* (1939) as the Wookie receives the same medal as the Cowardly Lion.

Schizophrenic design elements like these keep *Star Wars* visually interesting through its predictable plot. The "Alien Cantina" sequence, notorious for its inventive gallery of abominable creatures, might as well be Rick's from *Casablanca* (1942) after one too many highballs. The windows of the Death Star are geometric patterns of alternating metal slats—they look stylish enough but don't seem either aerodynamically sound nor practical for maintenance purposes. Luke, Han, and Princess Leia (Carrie Fisher) fight their way through Imperial storm troopers, computer wall circuits, and even a light-speed warp now and then, but their most daring escape, on a rope across a canyon of power generators, is straight out of *The Thief of Bagdad,* more than fifty years earlier.

Part of the reason *Star Wars* works so well is that Barry worked closely with Lucas to make the settings look old—none of that new-car look that dominated the spacecraft interiors of *2001.* The *Millennium Falcon* needs a paint job and a few screws tightened here and there. The garbage dump is full. Machinery is constantly breaking down or not working at all. The world is far from perfect. The settings tell us this is so, and the actors and the story are that much more enjoyable because they live in a realistic, if imaginary and time-less, world.

Enigmatic as well is *Blade Runner,* directed by Rid-ley Scott with production design by Lawrence G. Paull. Given the mediocre quality of Paull's other work (for example, *Cocoon: The Return,* 1988, and *Harlem Nights,* 1989), some of the credit for the film's incredible sets and effects must go to director Scott (*Alien,* 1979), art director David Snyder, special-effects supervisor Douglas Trumbull (*2001*), and Syd Mead, who is credit-ed as the "visual futurist," whatever that means.

Although set in a dark, perpetually rainy, and hope-lessly overcrowded Los Angeles of 2019, *Blade Runner* looks like—and obeys all the conventions of—a 1940s detective story, complete with the cynical, cigarette-smoking tough guy and the two-faced woman with whom he falls in love. Numerous production details point to a world of the future very much like the world of the past. Despite an evidently cold climate (people are constantly wearing rags of fur or huddling near open fires on the street), most of the offices are equipped with old-fashioned ceiling fans, as if all the power needed to run the computers and electronic surveillance equip-ment meant there was nothing left for central air or heat. Most of the buildings are leftover from archaic architectural styles, like the beaux-arts exterior of the Bradbury Hotel or the nonfunctional decorative embell-ishments of the facade of the Tyrell Office Building. Everything is lit by strobing neon or fluorescent lights, emphasizing the retrograde qualities of the settings.

Harrison Ford plays Deckard, a brooding ex-cop. (Characteristically, he has no first name.) He is the film's Humphrey Bogart. Sean Young plays Rachel (who has no last name), the ambiguously designed "replicant," or android, whom Deckard eventually comes to love. She is the film's Mary Astor. Most of the time, however, she dresses like Loretta Young, with a black, swept-up bee-hive hairdo and severe shoulder pads, leading us to believe that her creator, Tyrell, had a warm affection for forties film noir.

There are two characteristic visual images in the film, images that tell us the most about the production design. The first is the view of Los Angeles from the air, as seen by Deckard and his cronies in their "heli-car." The city lies choking beneath them, a haze of a million lights splayed up and down the sides of enormous build-ings. The continual rain reflects and obscures the details, leaving an image of exploding light; the only details to be picked out are the neon advertisements for Pan Am, Coca-Cola, Atari, Bulova, Budweiser, and TDK—all symbols of leisure and pleasure, all emblems of corporate control. The other characteristic image is the floating barge that wanders across the sky at key climac-tic moments during the film, such as our introduction to Deckard, the arrival of Rachel, and the final battle between Deckard and Roy, another replicant (played by Rutger Hauer). The barge is apparently some kind of junkmobile, in profile resembling a flying tank, disingen-uously disguised with advertisements for "off-world"

vacations or sensuous images of Oriental women eating. The horror and comedy of this machine, so outrageous and so bland at the same time, summarizes the condition of the entire city in the film, and thus the world.

Films like *Star Wars* and *Blade Runner*, filled as they are with images of the future that remind us so much of the past, serve the need for reassurance that every audience brings with it to the cinema—things will be really bad in the future, but no worse than they were in the past, in that mythical time and place that Hollywood invented in the first place. The films' relationship to the present is a little less formed, but prophecy and nostalgia have always been more popular than problem solving, and they are what science-fiction movies are all about.

Star Wars

The main rebel hangar—straight out of Flight Command *(1940). (Fox)*

SAGEBRUSH IN THE CORRAL: THE HOLLYWOOD WESTERN

Hollywood has always found the history of the West fascinating. Beginning with silent film star William S. Hart in 1914 and continuing unabated through today—with brief periods of neglect and revisionism—the Western has emerged as film's most popular and enigmatic genre. Its popularity is evidenced by the list of stellar names who have been attracted to the subject, while the enigma is evidenced by the endless interpretations of the Western's social, moral, and political significance.

The Western would hardly seem a likely place to encounter great art direction. The genre defines the setting, and the emphasis is almost always on character rather than production values. Yet Westerns have attracted their share of great designers, just as they have attracted great directors and actors who are willing to confront the challenge of creating a setting out of nothing but wood, sand, and sun and making that setting express something of the inner soul of the characters in the movie.

JOHN FORD AND MONUMENT VALLEY

The first revitalization of the Western, after a decade or so of cowboy serials, came with *Stagecoach* (1939), directed by

ABOVE: *Stagecoach*

The film company arrives at Four Corners, Arizona, in Monument Valley. (United Artists)

INSET: *Stagecoach*

The filmmaking hardware is gone, replaced by its nineteenth-century predecessor, the stagecoach. In the process, a passive space becomes energized. (United Artists)

John Ford. Ford had directed several silent Westerns, most notably *The Iron Horse* (1924), but he left the genre for thirteen years, until the right combination of story and setting came along. The principal setting for *Stagecoach*—and for the classic Ford Westerns to follow—is Monument Valley, an expanse of desert on the Utah/Arizona border. Characterized by flat, dusty basins interrupted every few miles by massive geological outcroppings, Monument Valley is both a blank canvas and an ideal shooting location. What more could a director, needing a mythic space for a mythic drama, want?

As with all of Ford's Westerns, the story of *Stagecoach* is simple, almost elemental: several passengers of different social classes are forced together to cross hostile terrain, aided by a reformed outlaw bent on a final act of revenge. The outlaw is the Ringo Kid, played by John Wayne in the role that made him a star, but many of the other cast members give equally impressive performances—Claire Trevor as the prostitute with a heart of gold, John Carradine as the last of the riverboat gamblers, Andy Devine as the simple soul, Thomas Mitchell as the doctor dependent on drink. To match these ordinary but archetypal folk, Ford needed ordinary but archetypal settings. *Stagecoach*'s art direction is credited

My Darling Clementine (1946)
Doc Holliday (Victor Mature) responds to a challenge by the sheriff, Wyatt Earp (Henry Fonda). (Fox)

to Alexander Toluboff, with Wiard Ihnen as his associate, but Toluboff was merely producer Walter Wanger's intermediary. Most of the work was done by Wiard Ihnen, a twenty-year veteran of five studios who had already worked with a dozen great directors before he was forty-five. Ihnen was originally a painter and never gave up painting. His beautiful sense of composition marks every frame of *Stagecoach.* Based on sharp contrasts of black and white, Ihnen's settings are perfectly suited to director Ford's vision of a West clearly divided into good and bad.

One excellent example of Ihnen's and Ford's felicitous use of natural and artificial scenery occurs early in the film, when the stage first leaves the town of Tonto. As the horses and passengers head out into the wilderness, we see the last, rough-hewn rails of the livestock fence in the foreground, with an endless and empty road stretching out before them, punctuated in the distance by one of Monument Valley's monolithic peaks. Similarly, later in the film, when Ford wants to show the attraction between the two outcasts, Ringo and Dallas (the prostitute), he frames them first in a dark hallway at the stage stop in Apache Wells, then in the outdoor courtyard, where a crumbling stucco wall and a lone cactus stand in for the desert night.

Ihnen's art direction is graphically simple, but combined with Ford's use of shadows, plunging perspectives, and tightly held close-ups reminiscent of silent-film style, it is not without significance. The word most commonly used to describe Ford's view of the West could thus equally apply to Ihnen's constructed sets and arranged landscapes: they are mythic, their meaning lying just below their familiar and classic surfaces.

Although it is unfortunate that Ihnen never got to collaborate with Ford after *Stagecoach,* this did provide the opportunity for one of Hollywood's most fruitful director/designer collaborations, that between Ford and art director James Basevi, who began his career as a special-effects designer; it was as the creator of the title effect in *The Hurricane* (1937) that he first came to work with Ford. Basevi was the sole or joint art director on nine Ford films, including the classics *My Darling Clementine* (1946), *Fort Apache* (1948), *She Wore a Yellow Ribbon* (1949), and *The Searchers* (1956). In all these films Basevi proved that he was singularly attuned to Ford's personal sense of individualism. He provided

Ford with a series of visual spaces in which Ford's larger-than-life characters could publicly act out their private battles.

Because it was the first Ford/Basevi collaboration, based on a popular legend, and centered by an outstanding performance by Henry Fonda, *My Darling Clementine* can be singled out among Basevi's great achievements in the Western genre. Basevi frequently worked with a collaborator; in *My Darling Clementine* it was Lyle Wheeler, who began his career with David O. Selznick and worked with William Cameron Menzies on *Gone with the Wind* (1939). Although nowhere near as dramatic as *Gone with the Wind,* Wheeler's work here with Basevi is just as extraordinary, for the two art directors succeed in giving an anonymous space in the middle of a natural universe a moral character and personality equal to that of the film's hero, Wyatt Earp (Fonda).

My Darling Clementine tells the story of Earp and his brothers, their alliance with Doc Holliday (Victor Mature), and their battle with the Clanton brothers, which culminated in the famous gunfight at the O.K. Corral. While the factual details have been scrambled for dramatic purposes, the heart of the story remains simple and true: Earp defends a dead brother's memory, falls in love with the pure and noble Clementine (Cathy Downs), but leaves her at the end to continue his vigilant crusade for Western peace and justice.

The centerpiece of the film's space is again Monument Valley. The valley frames the film as much as it frames the town of Tombstone, Arizona, where most of the action takes place. Within the moral quotation marks that the valley and its outcroppings create, Basevi and Wheeler have built a stage town in which the drama can be enacted. The heart of the town is the saloon, a room filled with thick, white smoke, the requisite tinkering piano, rows of gas lanterns, and framed boxing posters on the walls. The principal characters meet, drink, and wage war in this communal setting, an outpost of civilization in contrast to the endless and untamed space surrounding them. To further enhance the illusion of order, Tombstone also has a barbershop (the Bon Ton Tonsorial Parlor), a hotel (Mansion House), and a jail. But there can be no denying that these are bare hopes, something to retreat to when night, coyotes, and rustlers set upon the inhabitants of the town.

Never is the town's—and by implication, the towns-

My Darling Clemetine

The desert heat of Monument Valley means hats for
everyone during a break on the set. (Fox)

people's—precarious existence more graphically illustrated than in the scene of the camp dance in the unfinished church. Without enough funds to raise a roof, and only the barest rudiments of a bell tower (though they have the bell), the townsfolk of Tombstone thank the Lord and set to square dancing upon the nailed-down boards that constitute their church. The building is literally as well as figuratively a foundation for the future. Later, in the jail, Basevi and Wheeler make a virtue out of necessity in their use of low ceilings and dim-burning gas lamps. Of course, low ceilings were a way to save wood, and saving fuel was important, but their effect in the film is to make the characters seem uncomfortably close together despite the immensity of space around them, forcing them to rely on instinct and underlining the need for the moral and communal values that Ford holds so dear.

Even the town's name—Tombstone—is a constant reminder of the nearness of death. In the scene in *My Darling Clementine* where Fonda goes to visit his youngest brother's fresh grave, Ford shoots the headstone from so low an angle that it fills up half the screen, putting it on an equal footing with the hero. Thus in Ford's moral universe, a town can be a tomb, and a tomb can be a hero. Basevi and Wheeler did much to help Ford achieve his goals.

SHANE

John Ford was not alone among the great directors who were attracted at one time or another to the Western. Howard Hawks's *Red River* (1948) is one of the most acclaimed films in the genre, as is William Wellman's *The Ox-Bow Incident* (1943) and John Huston's *The Treasure of the Sierra Madre* (1948). Of these, Wellman's film had the most striking sense of design—the work of James Basevi again, this time in collaboration with Richard Day. Among the classic Westerns of Hollywood's golden age, one other film stands out as both a dramatic masterpiece and as a work of strikingly original design and visual beauty: *Shane* (1953).

Shane was directed by George Stevens, with art direction by supervisor Hal Pereira and associate Walter Tyler. Stevens was legendary for the care he gave his productions, often refilming and rewriting as he went along. For Stevens, in this case, Paramount Studios was the perfect match: the studio's vast wealth of props, veteran crew members, and rich heritage of perfection allowed Stevens to re-create the West of his dreams in extraordinary detail.

Most of *Shane* was filmed near Jackson Hole, Wyoming, where Pereira and Tyler and their crew built the Starrett homestead and the entire town to scale to make the action as realistic as possible. Crews watered the town's main street for hours to get it muddy enough for one scene, the fateful confrontation between Torrey (Elisha Cook, Jr.) and Wilson (Jack Palance). They rigged the victims-to-be with heavy-gauge wires so that their bodies would snap back dramatically whenever they got shot. As is typical of Paramount productions, special note should be made of the extraordinary contribution of the chief set decorator, in this film Emile Kuri. He took Pereira and Tyler's simple constructs and tricked them out with a profusion of accurate detail that is both pleasing to the eye and reassuring in the context of the story. In the Starrett home there is a blue-checkered tablecloth on the table, an iron stove topped with a griddle and kettle, needlepoint patterns draped over the simple wooden chairs, and a couple of delicious-looking fresh-baked pies. Equal attention is paid to the walls in Starrett's barn, the bar in the saloon, and the shelves of goods in the general store.

The heart of the story of *Shane* is not the battle between Starrett and the other homesteaders against Ryker and his gang, but the relationship between Shane (Alan Ladd) and Joey Starrett (Brandon de Wilde), and between Shane, Starrett (Van Heflin), and his wife, Marion (Jean Arthur). Since the characters' emotions are all strongly felt but hard to express, Stevens offers a scene early in the film in which the set works to telegraph their complex feelings for each other. It is Shane's first night at the house; he has gone to the barn to sleep. Joey heads to bed. The Starretts are getting ready to turn in. As each character passes through the central room of the house, he or she shouts out a goodnight to Shane. Joey wants to be the last to say goodnight. Mrs. Starrett looks longingly out of the top half of the front door, almost as if she would go out to Shane. Finally, all are in bed, bidding each other goodnight while the camera lingers over the dark and empty parlor, a symbol of the inexpressible yearning that connects and separates them.

Shane's greatest conceit, in relation to the art direction, is its ability to transform its settings into symbols and to use these symbols to express the emotions and aspirations of the characters in the story. Thus the town of Grafton, with its bones of civilization and the evil Ryker, is one icon; the Starrett homestead, representing the self-made man and his values of friendship and family, is another. The land in between—envisioned by Stevens as a range of white-topped mountains and wild game running free, where a man can do what he chooses—is a third icon. Tellingly, the film concludes with Joey chasing Shane from one icon to another, a codified rite of passage and a smaller version of the rite of passage that is, in fact, the entire film.

One footnote: we lack the full effect of the filmmakers' vision, for Paramount printed *Shane* on wide-screen stock before its release, against Stevens's wishes, thinking that mere Technicolor would no longer interest filmgoers. Despite this, the glorious colors of the majestic peaks and valleys are still intact, as are the muddy browns of the earth the men tried to cultivate and the streets and ditches they cleared to build their towns. Stretched or bleached, *Shane* still reverberates with grandeur and prompts us to reexamine the settlement of the West in the fictional and mythic setting that it always seemed to be.

THE REVISIONIST WESTERN

Although the Western film has never been unpopular, it went through a period of transition and reevaluation in the seventies and eighties from which a clear pattern has yet to emerge, if one ever will. The days of simple good men and unmitigated bad men are over. Luckily, the days of the bloodthirsty Indian are gone too. In their place has come a new interpretation of the national character, a soul-baring truth telling that often ends with the "white" man becoming the victim of his own ignorance or prejudice, or more existentially, with no resolution at all.

Two of the most interesting revisionist Westerns from a design point of view are Arthur Penn's *Little Big Man* (1970) and Robert Altman's *McCabe and Mrs. Miller* (1971). Both films had political agendas (Penn's more than Altman's), showing the history of America's westward expansion as one of despicable acts of violence, treachery, and stupidity (*Little Big Man*) or just laissez-faire morality (*McCabe and Mrs. Miller*). In their stead, they hoisted the dignity of the land and its native people as a model to the world. *McCabe and Mrs. Miller,* designed by Leon Ericksen, in particular showed the West as it probably really was: ramshackle, fly-by-night, and immoral. *Little Big Man,* covering one hundred years of American history and seen through the

Shane

*Shane (Alan Ladd) dancing with Marion
Starrett (Jean Arthur). The fence and the
mountains are real; the trees are fake.
(Paramount)*

eyes of one incredible witness, was designed by Dean
Tavoularis and Angelo Graham, and in retrospect seems
more in tune with Tavoularis's later *Godfather* epics
than with John Ford's parched spaces.

None of these films bears as much relevance now,
nor comments as directly on the nature and character of
the Western film genre as a whole, as *The Wild Bunch*
(1969), directed by Sam Peckinpah. *The Wild Bunch* is
a throwback to the classic Western, where a code of
honor and a good rifle were all a man needed to get by,
except that the gunfighters in this case are all pushing
fifty (if not way over it) and are eminently more moral
than the representatives of law and order they fight.
Additionally, there's no mistaking Peckinpah's trademark
slow-motion bloodletting for a Hollywood bullet wound.
These men are hurt, and bloodied, and die.

The Wild Bunch was designed by Edward Carrere,
who worked for Warner Brothers most of his career,
beginning with the ultramodern architecture for *The
Fountainhead* (1949) and including sleek thrillers
(*Dial M for Murder,* 1954), detective stories (*Sere-*

The Wild Bunch (1969)

The bunch in Mexico. From the left: Jaime Sanchez, Warren Oates, William Holden, Ernest Borgnine. (Warner Brothers)

nade, 1956), and musicals (*Camelot,* 1967). His easy-to-mold style must have appealed to Peckinpah, whose own personal stamp is notoriously hard to erase. Carrere designed several sets for *The Wild Bunch,* which, as realistic backgrounds to violence, add another element of verisimilitude to a film already rife with it.

Most astounding are the film's opening and closing set pieces, the sites of the bloody gun battles that frame the film and give it its reputation as the most violent Western ever made. *The Wild Bunch* begins in a small, well-settled south Texas town, circa 1913. The Mexican Revolution is raging just miles away, but the city's tree-lined streets, expensive lodgings, and rows of street-lamps testify to the frontier closing in these parts a long time ago. The temperance meeting taking place in the town square is another symbol of morality and stability. Into this placid setting, Peckinpah turns loose several gunmen of no particular allegiance. Dozens of innocent people are brutally shot and killed, often in slow motion. The West is a state of mind; it is never closed. The sub-urban setting only adds to the shock.

The bloody gunfight that ends *The Wild Bunch* is not set in the peaceful Texas town but in the midst of the Mexican Revolution. The town of Aqua Verde has seen many hardships; walls of crumbling bricks from demolished buildings shelter women cooking over open fires and children sleeping in tents. When the shooting breaks out, more innocents spill blood. Vultures fly into town. The senselessness and endlessness of the violence are pervasive, and though the wild bunch are dead we know the mercenaries and bounty hunters will be back another time, in another place.

Peckinpah's daring inversion of the clichés of the classic Western, combined with Carrere's treatment of sets that are both eternal and transitory, help make *The Wild Bunch* such a resonant and pivotal film. Its blunt visual style and dazzling montage (there are over five hundred shots in a little over two hours) are modern, while its treatment of men alone and the forging of moral values tie it to films like *Stagecoach* and *Shane.*

There is a scene in *The Wild Bunch* where one of the Mexican elders explains to Pike Bishop (William Holden), the leader of the bunch: "We all dream of being a child again, even the worst of us. Perhaps the worst most of all," and Pike remembers his life, full of impulsiveness and mistakes and roads not taken, and wishes the dream would come true. But the playful and watchful children who pepper the movie with their games and laughter are living proof that the past cannot be regained. The Old West, like childhood, is a memory. The stagecoaches, homesteads, and border towns of the movies are all that remain.

THE LURE OF THE EXOTIC: HOLLYWOOD ABROAD

Until television, motion pictures were the principal way to see the world, short of traveling. The world of the movies was a fantastic creation, equal parts cliché, incongruous detail, and unparalleled creative verve. National characteristics, customs, and even architecture were overemphasized and given a sensational slant in order to make a film more dramatic. In an era when in-studio productions were the norm for even the most far-flung places on earth, the art director more or less played God. Even now, when technological innovations have made outdoor work easier and the audience's taste for verisimilitude has made locations harder to fake, many filmmakers still prefer the controlled environment of the studio lot to the gamble of the real world. Factors such as the weather, international politics, equipment logistics, and cost all contribute to make location work an alternatingly tedious and terrifying activity.

There are two parts to the story of Hollywood abroad: that of the great art directors in the golden age, who built their cities of gold out of painted cloth and plaster, and that of the modern-day production designers, who rely on the actual location to contribute to the meaning of the film. The differences between the two are the differences between the old Hollywood and the new, between the innocence and idealism of the world in the thirties and forties and the cynicism and sophisti-

Lost Horizon (1937) Shangri-La: pristine, fantastic, modern, timeless. (Columbia)

TOP, LEFT: *Lost Horizon*

Director Frank Capra and art director Stephen Goosson working on a model of the set. (Columbia)

TOP, RIGHT: *Lost Horizon*

Cary Odell's sketch for the lamasery courtyard, duplicated to the letter for the film. (Columbia)

ABOVE: *Lost Horizon*

A studio employee, the model lamasery, and the tiny village below provide dramatic evidence of the game of scale the art department had to play. (Columbia)

cation that followed; in short, the difference between us then and now.

Most Hollywood films that take place in exotic locations rely on the convention of the misplaced outsider. This is the person with whom the audience can identify as he or she (usually he) tries to solve the mystery of his new surroundings. From Jack Conway in *Lost Horizon* to Rick in *Casablanca,* Holly Martins in *The Third Man,* T. E. Lawrence in *Lawrence of Arabia,* Colonel Willard in *Apocalypse Now,* and Jim Graham in *Empire of the Sun* (and including Sister Clodagh in *Black Narcissus*), the outsider has always undergone a trial in his new venue. This trial inevitably involves first disintegration, then inner strength, and eventually relief, if rarely triumph. The one element that these films share in addition to their exotic locales and their outsider hero is an ambiguous if not outright tragic ending.

LOST HORIZON

The first Academy Award that Columbia studios ever won for art direction was given to Stephen Goosson for his work on *Lost Horizon* (1937). This legendary film, directed by Frank Capra, is an example of Hollywood exoticism at its best. The overpitched realism during the escape from Bakul, the fateful flight into the Himalayas, and the crash and scavenging in the snow make a strange combination with the hypertrophied fantasy of Shangri-La. *Lost Horizon* maintains a glow of heartwarming joy even as many modern viewers laugh at it.

The winter scenes in *Lost Horizon* were filmed in a rented cold-storage warehouse in Los Angeles. The snow was real, as was the actors' frozen breath. These realistic sets, when combined with gray lighting, make a perfect pessimistic foil to the overly sunny and optimistic Shangri-La. For instance, the waiting room at the airfield at Bakul is a plain wooden box with loose-fitting windows, and the plane itself, while comfortable, is cramped and vulnerable. Once we get our first glimpse of the Valley of the Blue Moon (a miniature), the gritty realism of the prelude is abandoned as Goosson and his crew attempt to find the decorative and architectural correlative to the social idealism of the High Lama and his followers.

The exterior of the lamasery was built full-scale on a

TOP: *Lost Horizon*

*A sketch by Cary Odell for the native village. Odell would go on to be a major art director in his own right (*The Member of the Wedding*, 1953, and* The Caine Mutiny, *1954). (Columbia)*

ABOVE: *Lost Horizon*

It's a wrap! Stephen Goosson, Ronald Colman, Jane Wyatt, Frank Capra, and Isabel Jewell celebrate by sampling a cake model of Lost Horizon's *most famous set.*

Columbia lot in Burbank, California, the largest set ever built in California. Its design owes more to Frank Lloyd Wright's Imperial Hotel in Tokyo, built in the early twenties, than it does to actual Buddhist architecture, but it appears suitably grand and exotic from a distance. The interior, a time capsule of Western culture in anticipation of its eventual collapse, is like a museum. The rooms are austere—the sole decorations are oil paintings and an occasional objet d'art placed dramatically on a pedestal. The architectural style varies from the pseudo-Orientalism of the Chinese lacquer furniture and Japanese screens to the Art Deco window treatments. At one point the High Lama (played to perfection by Sam Jaffe) tells Jack Conway (Ronald Colman), "I determined to gather all things of beauty and culture I could, and preserve them here." One assumes that set decorator Babs Johnstone had to look no further than Columbia's property department.

Part of the silly fun of *Lost Horizon* comes from the huge gap that exists between the high idealism of the story and the naive images that accompany it. The High Lama waxes optimistically about the wonderful, carefree world he has created in Shangri-La, but we note that while he and his guests dine on fine crystal and silver samovars the natives in the valley have no running water and live in preindustrial thatched cottages. Likewise, it hardly seems desirable today to live in harmony with nature by paving it over with marble fountains and massive stairways, which make Shangri-La look more like a luxury hotel than a commune. Still, Goosson's sets are glorious, more dazzling if less cinematic than those of Cedric Gibbons or Van Nest Polglase. *Lost Horizon* stands alone as the epitome of Hollywood art direction at its most delightfully exuberant.

Lost Horizon

Inside a cold-storage warehouse in Los Angeles, studio technicians make last-minute adjustments to the Himalayas. (Columbia)

149

CASABLANCA

The "Casablanca" in *Casablanca* (1942) is a state of mind; nothing was actually filmed in French Morocco. This "Casablanca" is a place where no one can be trusted, where violent death or incredible acts of courage can occur at any moment. Its exoticness is entirely a result of this tenuousness and the air of desperation that envelops the people living there. The lure was freedom.

Casablanca has passed so completely into the realm of legend that it has developed its own mystique. Partly this is a result of happy accidents, such as the casting of Humphrey Bogart and Ingrid Bergman and the improvised ending of the screenplay, but surely some of the credit must go to the professionals who worked on the film, one of the most technically astute productions in Hollywood history. *Casablanca* was produced by Hal B. Wallis for Warner Brothers, thus assuring that unmatchable Warner's style of toughness, realism, and personal emotion that characterizes the studio's best work. Add to this the crackling screenplay by Julius and Philip Epstein and Howard

Koch, a cast of stars, Arthur Edeson's cinematography (he worked for Douglas Fairbanks on *Robin Hood,* 1922, and *The Thief of Bagdad,* 1924), and Max Steiner's score, and success is practically guaranteed.

The art director assigned to *Casablanca* was Carl Jules Weyl. For most of the thirties and forties, Weyl was the second choice in the Warner Brothers art department, behind Anton Grot. He was especially beloved by *Casablanca*'s director, Michael Curtiz, working with Curtiz on *Kid Galahad* (1937), *The Adventures of Robin Hood* (1938), *Mission to Moscow* (1943), and *Passage to Marseilles* (1944). He specialized in foreign locales and intrigues, making him ideal for *Casablanca.* Weyl also had the extraordinary assistance of set decorator George James Hopkins. Hopkins was, astoundingly, making his debut on *Casablanca.* His assurance shows in the manner in which the characters so convincingly

occupy his rooms, sit at his tables, and—from time to time—lift his glasses for a toast ("Here's looking at you, kid"). Hopkins's career lasted nearly thirty years; among his other stellar accomplishments as a set decorator are his dark and chilling interiors for *Strangers on a Train* (1951) and the extraordinary turn-of-the-century River City, Iowa, for *The Music Man* (1962).

The opening sequence of *Casablanca* establishes Weyl's mastery of the complex and exotic set. First we see the market street of Casablanca, with arabesques covering nearly every surface of the buildings, doorways, and gates. The camera pans down to introduce us to Rick's Café Américain in a compact sequence showing first the neon marquee, then the fancy lighting and tables, and finally the proprietor himself. Rick (Bogart) is a litany of icons now familiar to three generations of filmgoers—a martini glass, a cigarette smoldering in an ashtray, and a chessboard in midgame. Only at the end of the shot does the camera pan upward, away from the set and the set decorations, and show us Rick's face. The formal introduction is superfluous; Rick's surroundings have already defined him.

Similarly, Weyl's construction of Rick's Café does much to increase the mystery surrounding Rick and the citizens of Casablanca. Shadows are cast into the interior of the café—it is brighter outside than in. The perforated screens and Moorish columns throughout the spacious room hide as much as they reveal, and the thin wisps of smoke blowing around beneath the languorously spinning ceiling fans add to the element of concealment. The room is at once wide open and also very unsettling, almost tenuous—a fact we soon find out to be a true reflection of the mood of the majority of its patrons, European exiles trying to flee to neutral Spain. Reinforcing this juxtaposition of public faces and private desires, a searchlight continually fans across Weyl's sets, a reminder of Nazi tyranny and surveillance and as well a metaphor for the isolation of the individual.

The sets in *Casablanca* are utilized in a way that,

OPPOSITE: *Casablanca* (1942)

Rick (Humphrey Bogart) in front of his café, a publicity still not found in the film. (Warner Brothers)

Casablanca

A sheet of three set reference photographs of Rick's Café: top—the interior of the café; bottom left—a view of the bar; bottom right—Rick's office. (Warner Brothers)

later in the decade, would come to characterize film noir—ill lit, filled with shadows, and concealed by smoke and haze. Rick's apartment above the café is never more than partly seen (like Rick himself), content to remain a collection of vague shapes in near-total darkness—a window, white curtains, slatted blinds. Curtains separate Rick from the world, screens protect his patrons from the scrutiny of German officers, fog allows him to choreograph the elaborate ruse that ends the picture. And yet, in opposition to these constant barricades, there are windows everywhere, windows to freedom.

There is one scene in *Casablanca* where the setting loses its ambiguity and hints at the act of courage to come. Typically, the scene is a flashback to Paris, when Rick and Ilse meet in La Belle Aurore. Paris is under siege, but for the lovers the world has disappeared. The simplicity of the set, with the bar's exposed beams and

the red-checkered tablecloth on the table, proves it has nothing to hide. It is not Rick's. And Rick is not yet cynical. He is as simple as the room, and innocent. In this milieu we see Rick's potential for selflessness and his willingness to take risks, and are thus prepared for the end, when Rick sacrifices his love—and his café—for the greater good. *Casablanca* is many things to many people; now add a masterpiece of art direction to that list.

BLACK NARCISSUS

Black Narcissus (1947) was written, produced, and directed by Michael Powell and Emeric Pressburger, after Alfred Hitchcock and Alexander Korda the biggest names in British film history. It is one of the last, great masterpieces of entirely studio-based art direction. The

Black Narcissus (1947)

A holy man (Ley On) offers advice to Mr. Dean (David Farrar) and Sister Clodagh (Deborah Kerr) in front of one of Percy ("Pop") Day's magnificent painted backdrops. (Archers)

film was conceived from the start as a studio production. In his autobiography, *A Life in Movies,* Michael Powell wrote: "The atmosphere in this film is everything, and we must create and control it from the start. Wind, the altitude, the beauty of the setting—it must all be under our control." Based on Rumer Godden's novel of Anglican nuns given a mission to open a school and a hospital in the most remote region of the Indian Himalayas, *Black Narcissus* was filmed entirely in Surrey, England, on sets designed by Alfred Junge.

Junge's collaborations with Powell and Pressburger are among the most inspired and beautiful imaginary universes ever created for film. As a young man in Germany, Junge was thoroughly immersed in his nation's exacting design traditions. He designed films that were visually dazzling but lacking in soulfulness. It took a few years after his arrival in Britain in 1932 for the mitigating lessons of English romanticism to sink in. With *The Life and Death of Colonel Blimp* (1943), *A Canterbury Tale* (1944), and *I Know Where I'm Going* (1945), Junge, Powell, and Pressburger fashioned an extraordinary lyrical and reserved trilogy that stands uniquely apart in the history of British—and world—cinema. It remained for *Black Narcissus,* Junge's final collaboration with Powell and Pressburger, to extend this kind of beauty to an exotic and international scale.

The basic sets for *Black Narcissus*—the temple/convent in Mopu and the native village below it—were built full-size at the Archers Pinewood Studios, with vistas of the receding valleys and towering Himalayas painted onto canvas sheets by veteran British set artist Percy ("Pop") Day and his sons and then photographed behind the actors through a simple series of glass shots. Junge surrounded these sets with walls of planks painted with additional mountains and slanted backward at a 35-degree angle so that the midsummer sun would fall evenly across them all day, shadow free, thus increasing the amount of time Powell and Pressburger could spend shooting. This also guaranteed realistic, studio-controlled shadows in the completed film.

Junge's sets all serve the film's central conceit: that the nuns are apart from the world at the same time that they are in it. He decorated their convent at Mopu with dozens of bird cages, symbolizing confinement, and enormous windows, symbolizing freedom. There are constant reminders of the nuns' predicament, from the process shot showing the steep drop down from the courtyard bell to the valley floor, to the exotic Indian-style wall paintings and tiles left over from the building's days as a harem. The contrasts are most painfully evident in Sister Clodagh's flashbacks. Remembering a day before she took her vows, Clodagh (Deborah Kerr) can reconstruct, from one Proust-like moment involving a footstool, an entire room from her youth, down to the roaring fire, the yellow-shaded lamp, and the emerald necklace her beloved is offering her. In contrast to this,

ABOVE: *Black Narcissus*

Sister Clodagh (Deborah Kerr)
preparing to leave the temple.
(Archers)

LEFT: *Black Narcissus*

A model of the temple. Every foot
of the film was filmed at
Pinewood Studios, outside of
London. (Archers)

there are the beautiful but sterile gold and blue shadows that close over Mopu every sunset. The human dimensions of the story are subtly enhanced by the production design. Clodagh in effect admits this, near the end of the film, when she confesses to the other sisters, "I couldn't stop the wind from blowing and the air from being as clear as crystal, and I couldn't hide the mountain." Nature, internal as well as external, cannot be denied.

Powell, in his autobiography, wrote about how much he trusts silent-film technique. "In my films," he said, "images are everything . . . the ballet sequence in *The Red Shoes* [and] more than half of *Black Narcissus* are essentially silent films." Junge evidently knew this, and so he created visual equivalents to the sisters' emotions that tell the story as clearly as any lines of dialogue. In addition to those examples already mentioned, there is the main receiving room at Mopu, whose walls are intensely blue and covered with a red and gold stencil pattern and paintings that disturb the nuns so greatly that Clodagh demands they be removed, or the equally blue throne room laced with screens and lined with gilt-framed mirrors, and crowned with a glass bead chandelier under which a ridiculously exotic Jean Simmons sensuously dances.

In the end, the nuns cannot break the spirit of Mopu. Sister Ruth (Kathleen Bryan) perishes in a ghastly cliffside battle with Clodagh, and a flutter of birds, now free from their cages, signals the time for the sisters to leave the mountain. The rains come, the nuns depart, and the veil is dropped over this exotic land which merely stands in for the mystery of the human heart. *Black Narcissus* was the last gasp of studio-based production, and a romantic look at a world untouched by war.

THE THIRD MAN

Just as World War II came to a close, a shockingly original film came out of Italy. It was called *Roma, Città Aperta* (*Rome, Open City*, 1945), and it was directed by Roberto Rossellini. What was so shocking about *Open City* was its technique: shot on scraps of second-rate or doubly-exposed stock hidden from the Germans, filmed in Rome in the actual homes of many of the cast members (most of whom were not actors), the film was both a testament to Italian heroism and a blow to the old notion that films must be carefully planned and technically perfect to be successful. *Open City* was roughly cut, darkly lit, almost without music, yet it shone with an honesty, an integrity, and a kind of aesthetic brutality

TOP: *The Third Man* (1950)

A wary Holly Martins (Joseph Cotten) seeks the temporary shelter of a Viennese courtyard. (Korda/Selznick)

RIGHT: *The Third Man*

Holly Martins (Joseph Cotten) pursuing the crazed shadow of Harry Lime (Orson Welles). (Korda/Selznick)

that made it very moving, and an international success to boot. Hollywood, traditionally moribund when it comes to new ideas, reacted a bit coolly. It would take several more years and the more direct threat of television before realism would strike there, but from war-wracked England the response was direct and swift. It was *The Third Man.*

Carol Reed's masterpiece *The Third Man* (1950) is an early example of the power of location-based production, and a cynical look at a war-ruined world. Love, honor, patriotism, artistic integrity, ethics—all are either lost or unrecognizable in this film, directed by Reed, written by Graham Greene, and designed by the first genius of British art direction, Vincent Korda. Since 1936, when he blossomed in his brother's production of H. G. Wells's *Things to Come,* Korda had designed one magnificent film after another: the remake of *The Thief of Bagdad* (1940, in collaboration with the original designer, William Cameron Menzies), *That Hamilton Woman* (1941), and Reed's *The Fallen Idol* (1948). Now he turned to an entirely different kind of film.

The Third Man was filmed principally on location in Vienna. It tells the story of an American novelist who comes to take a job offered by a friend, Harry Lime, and

The Third Man

Postwar Vienna, 1950: not a documentary photograph but a still from the film. (Korda/Selznick)

gets caught up in a web of black-market dealings and murder. No sets could have re-created both the past glory and the present despair of Vienna. Korda's interiors are suitably seedy, such as the apartment where Lime (Orson Welles) lived, with its antique furnishings and quilts, or the striped wallpaper and wicker trim of the Casanova Club. But the star sets are the exteriors: the street where Lime supposedly gets run over, the Prater amusement park with its Ferris wheel-of-fortune, and the sewer where Harry and the novelist Holly Martins (Joseph Cotten) have their final encounter.

In *The Third Man* these exteriors are never too far away. In the opening scene, there are black marketeers selling watches and cigarettes in a public square. Piles of bricks and boards hold up the walls at Anna Schmidt's hotel. The statues are crumbling. At one point, Holly is chased by a pair of thugs through a hill of rubble. And then there's the sewer. All this literal detritus adds to the feeling of cynicism that the characters live and breathe in the film. As if the scenario and settings weren't disturbing enough, cinematographer Robert Krasker (with Reed's encouragement) tilted the camera in over a half-dozen of the film's key scenes to, in Reed's words, "suggest that something crooked was going on." This conceit gives the film's visual design a dazzling cinematic verve.

The freedom that working with actual exteriors gave to Korda and Reed spills over into a daring for unconventional effects in several interior sequences as well. For example, in one scene that takes place inside Anna's apartment, Reed's camera passes through a mesh of flowers sitting in a window, through the window, and down to the street below, where a person is nervously pacing. Then we see a cat running down the street, and the camera moves up and back to the apartment. It isn't until later that we discover that the person pacing is the supposedly deceased Harry, with the cat as his symbolic double, but the fluid visual movement through the scene enhances our feeling of imminent danger and vulnerability. Such camera mobility is usually impossible in a studio.

By far the most famous set in *The Third Man* is the sewer. Having run through the moral cesspool of postwar Vienna, the film fittingly concludes in an actual cesspool, as police from all the occupying forces, as well as Martins himself, chase Lime through a series of vast, dimly lit, flooded tubes. The actors themselves were not put through their paces in a real sewer, but Korda's perfectly tuned sets and the expert integration of location footage throughout the film make the point moot: this is where Harry's spirit is laid to rest. The burial of his body in the following scene is a mere postscript. Anna's final, unyielding rejection of Holly is one more cynical turn of the screw. As Anton Karas's plaintive zither music fades away, art direction in the British cinema reached a new zenith.

LAWRENCE OF ARABIA

The birth of the production designer, as a title distinct from the older one of art director, occurred as a result of the increasing complexity of filmmaking during the fifties. As special effects became more sophisticated and storytelling more realistic, tasks needed to be done above and beyond that of mere set design. This was especially true since, with the breakdown of the studio system, each project had to be developed from scratch. In addition, there was a rise in the amount and kind of location work required for a prestige picture. In the end, the production designer became the chief executive of the visual aspects of the film. No greater examples exist of the importance and power of the modern-day production designer than the three films that conclude this chapter—*Lawrence of Arabia, Apocalypse Now,* and *Empire of the Sun.*

Lawrence of Arabia (1962) was designed by John Box, who worked with the film's director, David Lean, on *Doctor Zhivago* (1965), and later with director Franklin J. Schaffner on *Nicholas and Alexandra* (1971). He has won four Academy Awards, the first two with Lean. His predilection for large-scale spectacle suited Lean perfectly; together Box and Lean give their films a visual scope and an almost abstract gigantism that have scarcely been equaled.

Lawrence of Arabia is so single-minded a pursuit of the life and times of Colonel T. E. Lawrence that despite its huge scale and three-hour length one can't help but recall it as a personal story. The dominant visual motif is that of Lawrence (played by Peter O'Toole) framed against a vast expanse of cream-colored sand. As a metaphor for Lawrence's individuality, this image is not only the motif for the film but a correlative of Lawrence's world view. Such philosophy is usually regarded as the

work of the director, but it is time to consider the contribution of Box, who, after all, helped select the locations, altered them to suit the needs of the crew, and filled them with truth-enhancing details.

Examples abound of Box's intervention in natural surroundings to add to the meaning of the film. Abstractions such as the first view of the desert, a strip of chocolate brown and pitch-black sand below a blazing orange rectangle of sunlight, or Lawrence and his men crossing the "sun's anvil" as a row of black dots inside a pair of dark and white inverted triangles (mountains and sand) reinforce the perception of the story as a blown-up parable of pure will persevering over pure nature. More "designed" sets such as the Arab encampment, with its hundreds of tents built upon a vast, mountain-ringed plain, or the attack on the Turkish train by a sweeping line of Arabs led by Lawrence are examples of

Lawrence of Arabia (1962)

The Arab army streams across the desert. No art director ever surpassed John Box's sense of epic and expansive scale. (Columbia)

157

the graphic simplicity of the film, a wise choice considering its lengthy narrative and complex morality. Compared to these understated but emotionally engaging set pieces, Box's most visually spectacular work, such as building a full-scale, exact duplicate of Aqaba in coastal Spain, seems ordinary.

The prototype for *Lawrence of Arabia* is partly the Western—with its solitary men and wide-open spaces—and partly Shakespeare, with Shakespeare's love of reducing national conflicts to personal journeys and defining victory as personal triumph. Is there any moment in *Lawrence of Arabia* more like *Stagecoach* (1939) than the one where Lawrence first leads his ragtag army into the desert, full of folly and unquenchable desire? And is there any moment more like *Macbeth* than the one, late in the film, where Lawrence surveys the ruined tanks, exploded bunkers, and bloodied bodies of his enemies as they spread out endlessly before him in the sand? The heart of great production design is seamless involvement in the story at hand—and this is it.

APOCALYPSE NOW

With *Apocalypse Now* (1979), we cross into the realm of controlled chaos as a method of filmmaking, where the circumstances of production mimic and even influence the final film. Directed by Francis Ford Coppola, with production design by Dean Tavoularis (the same team that produced all three *Godfather* movies), *Apocalypse Now* retells Joseph Conrad's *Heart of Darkness* as a tale of moral struggle in Vietnam. Colonel Willard (Martin Sheen) has been ordered to travel up a treacherous river to "terminate with extreme prejudice" a former Green Beret colonel named Kurtz (Marlon Brando) who has evidently gone insane and recruited a private army of acolytes. As Willard and his crew move up the river, the story becomes a reverse *Wizard of Oz:* Willard encounters more and more perversity and horror as he gets closer and closer to his goal.

In the years following the release of *Apocalypse Now,* rumors of utter despair, confusion, and sheer willfulness on the part of the crew and cast of the film have been more or less verified by the participants themselves, largely through Francis Coppola's wife, Eleanor, with her book *Notes* (1979) and the film *Hearts of Dark-*ness (1991). These documents merely underline our appreciation of the effort that went into this production.

By the time of *Apocalypse Now,* Coppola and Tavoularis had been working together more or less steadily for seven years. All the evidence points to a collaboration that is both intimate and exhausting. Tavoularis stayed with the director and the crew on location in the Philippines, helping to clear the jungles and build the villages while workmen built the temple decorations for Kurtz's compound from Tavoularis's sketches and photographs of the great temple of Angkor Wat in Cambodia. A hands-on designer, Tavoularis would climb into the Philippine rivers to arrange sampans for an aerial shot; he helped guarantee that the atmosphere of improvisation in the crew (by accident or by design) would extend to the sets.

Like *Lawrence of Arabia, Apocalypse Now* has elemental design themes that help reinforce the story—in this case, fire. Fire opens the movie, with the napalm bombing of a Vietnamese coastal village to the sound of the Doors' "The End," and—at least in the 70-mm version of the film—closes it, as Kurtz's compound is destroyed the same way. (Later and video versions of *Apocalypse Now* conclude with Willard leaving the compound; the credits run silently over a black background.) In between, there is firebombing from the air cavalry, streaming fire from burning houses, fire in buckets on the beach for a barbecue, fire on the roof of the boat heading up the river, fireworks at the Second Army camp, fire darts bursting out of the jungle, and finally fire to roast the slaughtered bull as Kurtz is killed.

The opposite of fire, of course, is water. The principal set of *Apocalypse Now* is the river, and as the characters frequently remark, the river is the only place where they are really safe. The few lighthearted, or at least ironic, moments in the film come as a result of one of Willard's men, Lance (Sam Bottoms), being a surfer, which allows him several opportunities to don shorts and grab a board. Even Kurtz, in one of his few moments of lucidity while lecturing Willard on T. S. Eliot, gently washes his face in a small bowl of cool, clean water. Both the use of fire and the use of water are production "business" that probably were imbedded in the film as a result of the director's and the designer's closeness; this is an excellent example of how small visual details can make enormous contributions to a film's ultimate impact.

At its most effective moments, *Apocalypse Now* is a hallucinatory nightmare. Piggybacked to the ever-confused Willard, the viewer is continually challenged to make sense of this violent, foreign place. It is hard to tell the good guys from the bad, enemies from friends, and especially good from evil. The screenplay, full of blunderbuss from so-called high-ranking military men like surf-crazy Kilgore (Robert Duvall), who loves "the smell of napalm in the morning," and outright black humor from civilians like Dennis Hopper's "photojournalist" ("I'm an American!"), adds to this confusion, as does the soundtrack—fragments of rock-and-roll music, unintelligible radio broadcasts, sirens, and Vietcong propaganda. Tavoularis's use of elemental effects such as fire and water, combined with visual set pieces such as the army camp that looks and functions like an amusement park, reinforces Coppola's message. Made in a time of moral confusion and abandonment, *Apocalypse Now* perfectly reflects its milieu.

EMPIRE OF THE SUN

Leave it to Steven Spielberg to produce a film that reduces the entire Second World War in the Pacific to a child's moral challenge. *Empire of the Sun* (1987) tells the story of a ten-year-old British boy, Jim Graham (Christian Bale), living with his wealthy family in Shanghai, and of the torture and degradation he endures when the Japanese conquer the city. He is separated from his family and sent to a prison camp. Like *Lawrence of Arabia, Empire of the Sun* centers around one brave individual's response to a new and exotic environment; like *Lost Horizon,* it posits the occasion for this response as a meeting between East and West. Only in this case there is not a trace of the sham Orientalism that makes *Lost Horizon* such a Hollywood museum piece. The life that Jim sees when he is forced out of his protective shell is brutal and uncontrollable.

Empire of the Sun was designed by Norman Reynolds, whose impressive credits include *Star Wars* (1977, for which he was John Barry's art director) and, recently, *Avalon* (1990). *Empire of the Sun* being a Spielberg production, Reynolds was very likely encouraged to think in a scope as huge as all humankind. *Empire of the Sun* was the first Hollywood production

Apocalypse Now

Francis Ford Coppola's and Dean Tavoularis's conceit of Vietnam as an out-of-control rock concert is implied in this still of soldiers hanging out on the scaffolding. (United Artists)

filmed on location in the People's Republic of China; most of the exterior shots of Shanghai and the English community there are the actual sites, tricked out with painted backgrounds and period details to make a more convincing transformation back to the forties. Reynolds and his team of five art directors, two chief set decorators, and four special-effects producers (plus the ubiquitous Industrial Light and Magic group) did a phenomenal job of re-creating the atmosphere of a world gone by, from the Georgian London village across the bridge from Shanghai, to the *Oliver*-like waterfront district of shacks and smoke, to the prairie prison filled with makeshift lanterns and pallets.

Realistic as they may appear to be, the sets in the film serve merely as window dressing. They are only important as to how they affect Jim, who holds the camera virtually every minute of this two-hour-plus film. Reynolds's mastery as a production designer is located exactly in his ability to create this detailed world and then make sure we recall nothing of it except as Jim experiences it, to make it personal, always a wise adage for a storyteller like Spielberg to follow. The most visually memorable moments in *Empire of the Sun* involve the transportation of the mundane and ordinary, if war-scarred, reality that surrounds Jim as it fills the screen with intensely personal imagery. For example, there is the scene that concludes the 1941 section of the film, just after Jim has been taken prisoner. Throughout the movie, Jim has been fascinated by airplanes and flying. Now, face-to-face with a real Japanese warplane for the first time, he walks right up to the workers welding it, becoming engulfed in its blue, hazy smoke and a constellation of red and orange metal sparks. Later, in 1945, as the American forces near Shanghai, we see Jim anxiously peering out of the window of his barracks as a sky show of spotlights, flares, and exploding bombs entertains him in the distance. Even the long shots of the sets, such as the airport hangar during the final Japanese counterattack, are seen explicitly from Jim's point of view, as he climbs up to the roof of the building and cheers the planes on, crying "Go, B-51, Cadillac of the sky!"

People travel to exotic places not only for the sake of travel but to learn something about themselves. This fundamental point is no different for Hollywood filmmakers in their treatment of foreign lands. Like life, sometimes the lessons learned are painful ones, such as that learned by Holly Martins in *The Third Man,* compelled to betray a friend, or by Jim Graham in *Empire of the Sun,* returning to his family but no longer a child. But a lesson about art direction in the cinema needs to be learned as well. The exotica of the East in *Lost Horizon* has nothing in common with the severity and discipline of the Japanese pilots during their sake ceremony in *Empire of the Sun;* the world has changed, and Hollywood—or what is left of it—has changed too. The audience has grown more intelligent, more cynical, and more willing to accept unvarnished truth, provided it's still packaged in an entertaining manner and has something worthwhile to say. What looks ridiculous, if charming, now in *Lost Horizon* then was merely innocence. The true horror of the settings of *Apocalypse Now* is that we so readily accept them. If only we could see with our old eyes again.

Empire of the Sun (1987)

The solitary journey of childhood: Jim Graham (Christian Bale) cycles down a street in war-torn Shanghai. (Warner Brothers)

THE LIGHT OF THE PAST: HOLLYWOOD AND HISTORY

Over the years, Hollywood's version of history has acquired a bad reputation. Every detail, from the buttons on the queen's collar to the firing speed of a flintlock rifle, has come under critical scrutiny at some point or another and come up wanting. On the whole the charges are well founded. The bottom line at the studios has always been profit, not accuracy. Yet for all its incongruities, Hollywood's history of the world is neither more nor less accurate than anyone else's. The film industry is subject to the same dialectic as everyone else: while trying to be as accurate as possible, people are limited by their own perspective and time in history. This was as true in the nineteenth century for Thomas Carlyle as it is in the twentieth for William Wyler. We can learn a little about the cultural life of the European ruling class in the sixteenth century by watching *The Sea Hawk*, but we can learn a lot about the clothing and furnishings of the forties by watching *Mildred Pierce* (1945).

In fact, *The Sea Hawk* and *Mildred Pierce* both were designed by Warner Brothers' top art director, Anton Grot. The challenge of history is a great temptation; most supervisory art directors have tried it once or twice. Grot handled Warner's sea epics as well as its noir dramas. Ken Adam made his reputation with James Bond before linking up with Stanley Kubrick for

The Sea Hawk (1940). The war in action: plotting England's demise in the Spanish Court. (Warner Brothers)

Barry Lyndon (1975). Norman Garwood went from the madcap *Brazil* (1985) to the sublime *Glory* (1989). Each art director, despite wildly divergent styles, was trying to be historically accurate. It is the definition of the word "accurate" that changed from decade to decade, not its goal.

THE SEA HAWK

The Sea Hawk (1940) captures veteran Warner Brothers art director Anton Grot at the height of his powers. Grot brought all he had learned about chiaroscuro lighting and suggestive spaces from his years with Douglas Fairbanks to the then-enormous $1.7-million budget to create perhaps the greatest studio-bound adventure film ever made. Every set in the film is overscaled and lavishly decorated to match the larger-than-life battle between great men and great nations in the story. The Spanish Court is filled with elaborately carved oak chairs and a wooden table at least 40 feet long. The walls are covered with decoratively framed oil portraits and ringed with silver candlesticks, and the floors are of highly polished marble. This is only the first scene.

As the action continues, Captain Geoffrey Thorpe (Errol Flynn) and his men lead us across the English Channel—actually a 12-foot-deep lake built on a new sound stage by the studio especially for this production—into the English palace, and eventually into Queen Elizabeth's own private chamber. Her Majesty's 10-foot-high fireplace, dark tapestries, and few scattered pieces of deeply carved wooden furniture get lost in the banquet hall–size room. *The Sea Hawk* is full of small touches like the graphic tangle of ropes, swords, and poles as Thorpe's "Albatross" and the Spanish galleons fight to the death on their full-scale sets in Warner's lake, or the magnificent royal garden in Spain, where Thorpe woos Donna Maria Alvarez de Cordoba (Brenda Marshall). The piles of flowers and the elegant, sculpted trees in the garden are photographed by the masterful Sol Polito in such a way that their reality and the inevitability of the two lovers' happiness seem to be twinned natural phenomena.

Glimpses of Grot's use of dramatic lighting effects to mask undefined settings occur in the scene in which Thorpe is imprisoned on the Spanish galleon. Nearly the

The Sea Hawk

Queen Elizabeth (Flora Robson) sees Captain Geoffrey Thorpe (Errol Flynn) and his entourage off to battle. (Warner Brothers)

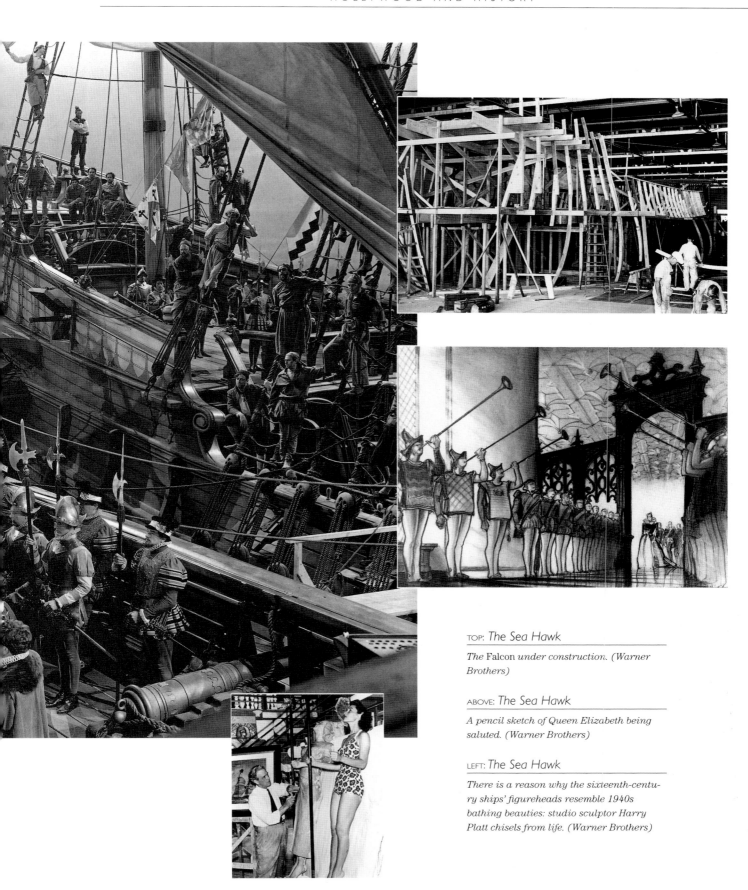

TOP: *The Sea Hawk*

The Falcon *under construction. (Warner Brothers)*

ABOVE: *The Sea Hawk*

A pencil sketch of Queen Elizabeth being saluted. (Warner Brothers)

LEFT: *The Sea Hawk*

There is a reason why the sixteenth-century ships' figureheads resemble 1940s bathing beauties: studio sculptor Harry Platt chisels from life. (Warner Brothers)

entire screen is black, filled with the darkness and oppression of the setting; only a few spots of exterior light fall upon the naked upper torsos of the prisoners and, tauntingly, on the iron gate and steps leading to the deck and freedom. Such intimacy and stillness provide a needed and invaluable contrast to the inevitable furor when the deck fills with shimmering sunlight and rioting Englishmen.

The greatest of the settings in *The Sea Hawk* come near the end, after Thorpe has escaped and sneaked back into England to warn his queen of her advisor's treachery. In a magnificent dramatic sequence, Thorpe arrives in the rain at the dark, cobble-stoned gate of the English Court and proceeds one step ahead of his pursuers through the stone hallways and candlelit chambers of the palace. Inevitably he is cornered, whereupon commences one of the famous Flynn sword fights (this time with Henry Daniell as Lord Wolfingham, a fictitious take on Francis Walsingham, Elizabeth's secretary). The two soldiers scramble up and down the stone stairwells, overturn a music stand and a table, and eventually burst through a stained-glass window and finish their duel in the throne room, nearly on the queen's lap. Not only is this excellent drama, it is also a great way to show off every inch of the set.

One of the grand conventions of old Hollywood, not too much in use these days when realism must be extended to the absolute limit, was to invite the entire cast to the sound stages for the last scene of the picture,

bringing with them as many pieces of property as would fit. *The Sea Hawk* features one of the greatest of all sendoffs, literally as well as figuratively, as Elizabeth (Flora Robson) bids farewell to Thorpe as he prepares to lead a force against the Spanish, surrounded by the two full-scale rigs and every extra available on call. Victory for all is assured.

BEN-HUR

No one is as sensitive to the irony of stories about the rise and fall of great empires as Hollywood. The biblical epic has attracted big-screen adherents since D. W. Griffith's *Judith of Bethulia* (1914) and *Intolerance* (1916). Although they still turn up every now and then, the popularity of the genre seems to have crested in the fifties, simultaneous with the demise of the Hollywood empire itself. Stunned by the success of television, reeling from regulations that turned their mighty legions of theaters into fractured, independent entities, Hollywood studios made several last-ditch attempts to overwhelm the American people with their ability to entertain. Perhaps the greatest of these attempts, and certainly the grandest in regard to the art direction, was William Wyler's *Ben-Hur* (1959).

The figures, in this case, prove useful: over three hundred sets covering more than three hundred acres, eight thousand extras, over one thousand employees working on one set alone—the arena for the legendary chariot race. The total budget was nearly $13 million, even though most of the film was shot in Italy, where the landscape already resembled Palestine and the Cinecittà studios were cheaper to rent than Hollywood locations. Everything about *Ben-Hur* was epic—even the story. Hollywood may have been emotionally bankrupt by this time, but it sure was going to prove a trouper on the way out the door.

The art directors who worked on *Ben-Hur* were William A. Horning and Edward Carfagno, with special photographic effects by A. Arnold Gillespie. Horning and Gillespie were veteran MGM employees; their association went back twenty years to *The Wizard of Oz* (1939). Carfagno came up through the ranks at MGM and began his career as an art director in the forties. His credits include musicals such as *Good News* (1947) and *The*

The Sea Hawk

A rare late Anton Grot sketch. (Warner Brothers)

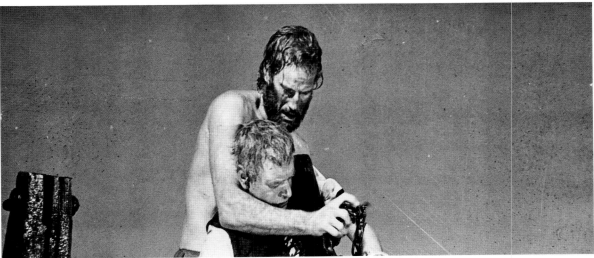

Barkleys of Broadway (1949) as well as a warm-up for *Ben-Hur, Julius Caesar* (1953). In a production of this size, Horning, Carfagno, and Gillespie probably spent most of their time managing the sets and crews, leaving the actual designing to their staffs. This may account for the feeling throughout the lengthy film of sheer spectacle overriding emotional intensity. Although not without its dramatic moments, the narrative of *Ben-Hur* pales in comparison with its visual scope and splendor. The enormity of the settings prohibited the kind of indefinable comfort and familiarity a smaller but more integrated production would have allowed.

Emotional content aside, several of the set pieces in *Ben-Hur* provide the kind of visual wallop for which Hollywood is famous. The primitive elegance of Judah Ben-

Ben-Hur (1959)

This pair of photographs illustrates the consummate artistry of A. Arnold Gillespie: a live action shot of Judah Ben-Hur (Charlton Heston) saving Quintus Arrius (Jack Hawkins) with the background matted out, and the miniature galleys and painted sky to match it in the completed film. (MGM)

Hur's house in Jerusalem, with its inlaid marble floors, pierced wicker-screen windows, and luxurious "couch" covered with needlepoint pillows, more resembles the Victorian painter Lawrence Alma-Tadema's view of the ancient world than anything that might have been found at Hadrian's villa. Likewise, for the homes of Jerusalem, already with stone towers, stone doors, and embossed stone plaques, the art directors might be said to have gone too far in having stone awnings as well. But it should be recalled that the story of *Ben-Hur* is, after all, based not on the Bible but on a novel by Lew Wallace that was still popular when Louis B. Mayer was an impressionable boy. It is easy to see why Victorian exuberance and not Roman stoicism was the order of the day.

The two most famous of *Ben-Hur*'s epic scenes are the sea battle and the chariot race. The sea battle was the work of the great Arnold Gillespie, now in the last few years of his career. Through a combination of miniatures, rear projections, and full-scale sets, Gillespie managed to capture the frenzy of naval war in the age of Rome in startlingly realistic detail. The studio had to match action shots of the actors struggling with the flaming catapults and engaging in very real fisticuffs with miniature models of the boats in a studio tank, complete with ramming oars and splintering decks, and the whole then had to be lit and filmed to maximum effect and edited at such a pace that any inconsistencies would be masked—a magnificent triumph for a craft soon to be transformed by technology.

Very little was miniaturized in the climactic chariot race. The arena was completed to scale and filled daily with thousands of roaring extras; only the views of the hills of Jerusalem in the far background were painted. The giant statues of the Roman gods that fill the inner circle of the racetrack were built by Italian sculptors in realistic approximation of the originals. These statues actually have the best view of the race, as the camera repeatedly assumes their point of view. Andrew Marton was hired to direct the race sequence due to his experi-

ence in action films, and the mobile cameras capture the excitement of the battle between Ben-Hur (Charlton Heston) and Messala (Stephen Boyd) with the immediacy of a live event. This is a classic example of an instance in which the scale of the settings was entirely appropriate and used to great advantage to heighten the dramatic value of the scene.

As the message of *Ben-Hur* grows more portentous near the end, the film's decor becomes a bit frozen in its grandeur—nothing equals the sheer exuberance of the earlier action sequences. From the symmetrical elegance of Pilate's palace in Jerusalem to the classical half-circle of the trial arena, the Victorian elements take over from the more genuinely rugged Roman ones. With the Crucifixion and the healing of Miriam and Tirzah, *Ben-Hur* ends a little too neatly, but the view was glorious from beginning to end.

A MAN FOR ALL SEASONS

Many historical films have a hidden agenda, some element—other than the accidental references to contemporary costume or decor—that links them to the time in which they were made. *The Sea Hawk* subtly links Britain's fate in the war with Spain with its then-current tribulations with Germany. *Ben-Hur* can be seen as a parable of the modern-day empire of America, as proud and imperiled as ancient Rome. In the sixties, historical drama took a deeply personal turn, concentrating on individuals (*Tom Jones,* 1963), intimacies (*Anne of the Thousand Days,* 1969), or eccentrics (*Marat/Sade,* 1967). In addition, the increased sophistication of the moviegoing public demanded a more detailed and unified treatment of history than Hollywood was used to giving, and this desire for naturalism poured over into the production of historical epics. Most emblematic of this new naturalism is Fred Zinnemann's production of Robert Bolt's play *A Man for All Seasons* (1966). The film tells the true story of Sir Thomas More, who was condemned to death for refusing to sanction the authority of the king of England, Henry VIII, over the pope. Yet for all of its high ideals and upper-echelon politics, *A Man for All Seasons* is a surprisingly intimate film.

A Man for All Seasons was designed by John Box, one of the most preeminent film designers of the sixties,

OPPOSITE: *Ben-Hur*

The road to Lepers Valley. MGM was one of the last studios to build detailed exterior sets. (MGM)

A Man for All Seasons (1966)

Spiritual chaos versus temporal order: production designer John Box provides Sir Thomas More (Paul Scofield) with sets filled with rhymed squares and opposed by rows of faceless churchmen. (Columbia)

fresh from his successes in *Lawrence of Arabia* (1962) and *Doctor Zhivago* (1965). As suggested by the title, natural elements play a large—if not the main—part in the design scheme of the film. Sir Thomas (Paul Scofield) is seen continually riding up and down the river that flows almost literally from his doorstep to the king's palace in London. The river is seen at its most beautiful in the budding spring, when Thomas's fortunes are high, but it is also seen in the dark of winter, when Thomas's tide is low and no one in the king's employ will even bring him a boat to take him home. The purity, silence, and eternal flow of the river is a good match to the straightforwardness and honesty of Thomas's character, especially when contrasted to the king and his court, who are usually introduced by stone. Parliament is a large stone room, ringed by stone benches; the tower is made of white stone, and at Cardinal Wolsey's home stone statues greet his visitors. Indeed, images of stone gargoyles open and close the film, symbols of the soullessness of Thomas's antagonists, and of their triumph. Ironically, the water and the endless cycle of nature, even in defeat, seem hopeful, while Thomas's persecutors, in their intransigence, resemble stone.

Box's settings are generally more understated than would be expected, as if he were translating T. E. Lawrence's Arabian asceticism to Sir Thomas More's own chambers. The scale of Thomas's Tudor home is certainly grand, but the furnishings and decorations are austere. Not that the royal chambers or the halls of the church are much more exotic—stone pillars and red rugs are the usual backdrops to the actors. This reticence can be explained partly by the source material—a play—and partly by the times—the mid-sixties, when the extravagance of riches and the lives of the rulers had to be scaled down to human proportions to be accepted. But there is a third factor involved, one that makes *A Man for All Seasons* more than a filmed play or a spiritual exercise, and that is John Box. Having seen Box at work in *Lawrence of Arabia*, we know that he had the profound ability to transform raw space into poetry, and that is precisely, with a bit more detail, what he does with his settings for *A Man for All Seasons.* As in life, the space surrounds the man—Sir Thomas—and defines him, sometimes with his knowledge, sometimes without it.

No clearer example of this can be seen than during the trial. Thomas has been brought up on some minor charge, so the king can have him convicted and executed and proceed with his plans to marry unimpeded by Rome. The outcome is known by lawyer, king, and counsel, yet the most eloquent statement is mute, made by the setting, and vindicating Sir Thomas: above the red-robed judges, conspicuous to all, hangs the royal seal. But there's a window above the royal seal, towering over it, and through that window, clearly visible, is the sky. Man's domain ends on earth, but God's penetrates all the way to heaven.

BARRY LYNDON

The period film as formal exercise reached its zenith in *Barry Lyndon* (1975), written and directed by Stanley Kubrick and based on William Makepeace Thackeray's novel. Barry Lyndon (Ryan O'Neal) is a farmer's son who, through luck and deceit, works his way up to the very top of eighteenth-century English society, only to suffer a series of disastrous reversals and end up crippled and as poor as he began. With the same sense of outrageousness that he brought to his earlier masterpieces *2001: A Space Odyssey* (1968) and *A Clockwork Orange* (1971), Kubrick basically ignores the story (or stretches it out and slows it up in a manner that makes it wholly undramatic) and concentrates instead on presenting his film as a series of visual tableaux that function as captions.

Barry Lyndon was designed by Ken Adam, who made his career with James Bond. The tongue-in-cheek shenanigans of *Doctor No* (1962) and *Goldfinger* (1964) were no preparation for the icy logistics of *Barry Lyndon*, but then again no art director comes out of an encounter with Stanley Kubrick unchanged. Kubrick and Adam spent several years in preparation prior to production. Kubrick put together a picture file, and Adam studied British history painting and Georgian architectural detail.

The film is full of examples of deliberately overstudied design. Repeatedly, Kubrick will begin a shot in close-up and pull back slowly to reveal the scene, such as the early shot of the lines of Redcoats drilling in an Irish field. The formal exercise of the soldiers precisely mimics the formal exercise of the filmmaker: a series of lines (soldiers) marching in a square while the aperture of the lens pulls back to frame them in an ever-larger series of rectangles (the screen). If this sounds a bit precious on the page, go look at the sequence in the movie. Such linear qualities may be abstract in the description, but they are luscious to look at.

Adam's use of graphic and painted landscapes to frame the action is also pivotal to the look of the film. The graphic landscape is used in *Barry Lyndon*'s frequent traveling episodes. As Barry crosses a field or rides in the country, his surroundings are turned into a frame, their lines leading him to his fate. Such graphic landscapes are also used occasionally for interiors, such as the reception for the king, where the deeply receding perspective and the noble receiving line into which Barry has uneasily fit emphasize the restrictions placed on the individual in eighteenth-century society and Barry's inability to accommodate himself to them. In contrast, the painted landscape does not move: it echoes the Thomas Gainsborough portraits and Thomas Rowlandson landscapes upon which Kubrick initially based his ideas. Sometimes during *Barry Lyndon* it seems the camera moves more than the actors, most notably in the gaming room in Saxony where the light, the clothes, and even the color of the walls are such a gorgeous shade of vermilion that the production seems to have come to a standstill to observe them. The entire film is really a sequence of painted landscapes linked by graphic landscapes. Several other scenes are noteworthy: the card game in the Lyndon drawing room, with the countess (Marisa Berenson) immobile behind a fan of playing cards, her maids rigidly at her side, or a concert on the lawn in which, until it is broken up by Barry's drumbanging son, one can nary find evidence of breathing.

In his desire to be faithful to the book and also to leave something of a document of his own turbulent

Barry Lyndon (1975)

In his sets production designer Ken Adam imitated the sweeping scale and formal serenity of classical British landscape painting. (Warner Brothers/Peregrine)

times, Kubrick has made *Barry Lyndon* into one of the most beautiful and sensuous descriptions of an absolutely uncontrollable and unyielding hell. This hell is the modern world, into which Barry Lyndon as Everyman cynically attempted to ingratiate himself and from which he was as equally and cynically disgorged.

AMADEUS

Amadeus (1984) is the whitest movie ever made. From the beginning, with the streets of Vienna blanketed by snow, to the end, with the powdery white lime being tossed into the grave of Wolfgang Amadeus Mozart, *Amadeus* is an homage to every emotion associated with the color white—unobtainable purity, the abstract notion of a benevolent God, and natural harmony. In the course of the movie, we see a white ballroom; hundreds of white wigs; white stone walls in the asylum where Mozart's rival, Antonio Salieri, has prepared to die; the child Mozart in a white suit, playing the harpsichord blindfolded; the white walls with gilded stucco of the prince archbishop's palace; the emperor's court where Mozart makes his appearance in an outrageous and oversized white hat; and a series of white pierced screens on the stage of the Vienna Opera House. This is only in the first forty minutes.

Amadeus was directed by Miloš Forman, and a good part of the sensational success Forman had integrating this florid fantasy into the real world of late-eighteenth-century culture and politics comes from the fact that most of the film was shot on location in Czechoslovakia, Forman's native country, with an entirely Czech crew. This was not an exotic locale for them, but their home and their heritage, and the acuity they brought to the production mitigates the obvious Hollywood attributes of the film's stars, Tom Hulce as Mozart and F. Murray Abraham as Salieri. The film's production designer, Patrizia von Brandenstein, who began her career as a costume designer (like *Blue Velvet*'s Patricia Norris), supervised two separate crews, one in Prague led by art director Karel Czerny, and another in Italy led by art director Francesco Chianese. For some reason only Hollywood would know, Czerny and Chianese took home the Academy Award for their work, not von Brandenstein,

despite the fact that Chianese's billing came in the middle of the credit crawl for the much smaller Italian crew, while von Brandenstein's came right at the top. Additionally, Forman hired another designer, Josef Svoboda, to do the opera sets.

With all these international arrows pointing in different directions, one would think that *Amadeus* would be a visual mess, but in fact it is an extremely unified and coherent production. In addition to the ubiquitous whiteness, *Amadeus* has an elegantly designed sense of space. Salieri, who has grown old, is trapped in a hospital chair and sealed in a hospital room; all his life he has longed for Mozart's freedom and irresponsibility. Mozart, on the other hand, is running for his life. His first appearance in the film as an adult shows him running the entire length of the prince archbishop's massive, high-ceilinged hall to get to his music, and he doesn't stop running, figuratively, until he dies. This sophisticated sense of space can be found also in Forman's and von Brandenstein's use of the opera sequences as mirrors held up to the glittering unconventionality of Mozart's life. The few glimpses of stagings we get to see, such as the crumbling brick walls in *Don Giovanni* or the bouncing scenery in *The Abduction from the Seraglio,* seem no more outrageous or ridiculous than the rows of bewigged citizens facing them or the dandified revelers at a costume ball. Mozart's world is a fantasy facing a fantasy, and *Amadeus* shows us how easy it was for the great composer to conclude that all of life was meant to be his subject and his stage.

The most glorious sequence in *Amadeus,* however, is not white, nor is it dramatically staged. It is the penultimate one, where Mozart on his deathbed dictates his Requiem Mass to the alternatingly astounded and mortified Salieri. Actually, there is a little bit of white, for there are white candelabras framing each rotating shot, as Mozart verbalizes a chord or two (which the soundtrack thunderingly re-creates) and Salieri scribbles it down. This scene may not have much in the way of art direction, but it does capture the genius and tragedy of artistic creation as few sequences in any Hollywood film have ever done. The art direction returns soon enough, with white-liveried soldiers standing guard over the gates of Vienna as Mozart's wife rides into the city to see him one last time—and then that shower of white lime to wash away Mozart's body once his soul has gone to heaven.

GLORY

Hollywood always seemed to portray the history of distant and foreign lands with more acumen than its own. Too often, films about American history turn into patriotic lectures or trivial love stories. *Glory* (1989) is an exception, neither being terribly patriotic nor containing the slightest hint of romance. In short, *Glory* is one of the purest, least sentimental, and most intimate war films ever made.

Directed by neophyte Edward Zwick (among his few other credits are *About Last Night,* 1986, and television's "thirtysomething"), *Glory* is the true story of the Fifty-fourth Regiment of Massachusetts, the first all-black combat unit of the Civil War, and of their training and eventual action under the command of their white colonel, Robert Gould Shaw (Matthew Broderick). The production was designed by Norman Garwood, whose earlier masterpiece, *Brazil,* has absolutely nothing in common with *Glory*'s elegiac visualizations of the horrors of war.

Autumnal colors dominate the screen, as befitting the somber subject. The Readville Camp, where the new recruits receive their earliest training, is a smoky, brown landscape, flecked in the darkness by orange fires and bolts of rusty iron. Rain is falling, obscuring and at the same time idealizing the landscape. Later, in their first battle on James Island, South Carolina, the lines of the blue Union soldiers and the gray Confederate ones merge amid the brown, wooded battlefield in shot after shot of medium range, so that one cannot get a handle on the plan or pattern of the fighting but only take away the memory of a senseless clash, abstract and unnatural. Zwick composed *Glory* almost entirely of close-ups and medium shots, forcing Garwood's already understated settings even farther into the background. When remembering the film, few specifics remain, only a general haze of burning buildings, muddy tents, and darkness.

The design of *Glory* also contains a spiritual element. There are no generals in this war film, no battle plans, no political maneuvers. The focus is kept entirely on the men, especially the black men. They have been forced into a new social situation and a world of infinitely more freedom and danger than they ever knew before. The low singing in the camp and the pre-battle speechifying are one signal that these men are preparing to meet their Lord. There are also visual clues. In the attack on Fort Wagner, an attack that will surely kill many of the men and ultimately will not even succeed, Garwood simplifies the setting until there is nothing between the men and their destiny but a strip of tan sand. As the battle begins, blue smoke settles over the field, again preventing us from seeing the action as a piece of history, forcing us to see it instead as the efforts of individual men. The end is intense, bloody, and intimate. Shaw is killed; the battle lost. But in the final image of the dead Union soldiers being piled into mass graves, white and black together, something stronger than victory is won, something like righteousness.

Hollywood has come a long way from the poetic racism of *The Birth of a Nation* (1915) to the poetic fraternity of *Glory,* and yet not as much progress has been made as has been imagined. The visualization of history is still fraught with the maker's baggage, and we are no closer to perfection now than we have ever been. In fact, if there is one lesson Hollywood history films have taught us over the years, it is that we have not learned a thing. The English fools who listened to the Spanish lies will listen to the German lies as well. Jews can be blamed and punished in America as in Galilee. Sir Thomas More was chastised and eventually murdered because he refused to cut the cloth of his conscience, as many would again. Barry Lyndon's opportunism still appeals, and still fails. Like Salieri, we still do not understand God's purposes. And like Colonel Shaw, sometimes we have to die to prove ourselves right.

LOST INNOCENCE: ART DIRECTION AND ALFRED HITCHCOCK

In the sea of Hollywood, Alfred Hitchcock was the shark who swam alone. He never associated with any one studio, preferring instead to negotiate separate and increasingly favorable contracts on a per-film basis. He was the first Hollywood director whose name was recognized by the moviegoing public, and the first whose films were linked with one particular genre: suspense. But there is one aspect of his career that is more relevant here than his independence or his notoriety: Hitchcock designed his own films.

Hitchcock was born in England and began his career in film designing the title-card drawings for the British branch of the Famous Players/Lasky company. Later he gained invaluable experience working for director George Fitzmaurice, and he spent some time in Germany working with director F. W. Murnau, from whom he learned important lessons regarding expressive film lighting and the economy of storytelling. When the Lasky company closed down its English operation, Hitchcock teamed up with producer Michael Balcon, receiving credit for the art direction on five films.

By the time of his first sound film, *Blackmail* (1929), Hitchcock had more or less perfected the design technique he would utilize for the rest of his career. Before production began, he would sit down with the screenplay and write out

Foreign Correspondent (1940) *The assassination of Van Meer's double, with sprinklers visible overhead and klieg lights ringing the false walls. (United Artists)*

storyboards with crude stick figures illustrating the positions of the actors and the camera as well as the frame of the setting for every scene in the film. The actual designing of the sets and the time spent filming them were fairly anticlimactic so far as Hitchcock was concerned; for him all the creative work had occurred on the storyboards. Although Hitchcock never claimed screen credit for the art direction on any of the films he directed, the evidence is overwhelming that he personally supervised the work on all of them, changing things to suit his needs, making suggestions to the art department in mid-production, and familiarizing himself with every detail of the set.

Through the sheer power of his personality, Hitchcock managed to work at one time or another with most of the major studio art directors. For *Rebecca* (1940) he drew Lyle Wheeler, then working for David O. Selznick; for *Suspicion* (1941), with RKO, Van Nest Polglase and Carroll Clark. *Rope* (1948) has Perry Ferguson as art director, and *Dial M for Murder* (1954) has Edward Carrere. And that's not counting the trio included here, men whose instinct for telling detail and willingness to adapt their style made them Hitchcock's most perfect matches: Alexander Golitzen, Robert Boyle, and Hal Pereira.

FOREIGN CORRESPONDENT

When the winds of war began to blow in Europe, Alfred Hitchcock chose to make another espionage film in the style of his earlier success, *The 39 Steps* (1935). Working with independent producer Walter Wanger and independent art director Alexander Golitzen, Hitchcock and his writers (who included Charles Bennett, James Hilton, and Robert Benchley) fashioned a tale of romance and intrigue involving an American reporter (Joel McCrea), the supposed peace negotiator he's investigating (Herbert Marshall), and the negotiator's daughter (Laraine Day), with whom the reporter falls in love.

Although Hitchcock disliked location work due to the lack of control he had over lighting and backgrounds, he equally despised the canned look of a studio interior. Luckily, he had the financial clout to get what he wanted, which was usually a studio-built set scaled to outdoor

work. *Foreign Correspondent* is no exception: it has almost one hundred fully built sets, including a city square in Amsterdam, a three-story windmill, and a 600-foot version of Waterloo Station. In the scene filmed in the square, the site of the Van Meer assassination sequence and the ensuing chase through a sea of umbrellas, so much water was consumed that the Colorado River had to be diverted to accommodate the picture's demands. For the realistic plane crash, Golitzen built an entire airplane, with a 120-foot wingspread and nearly 100-foot fuselage, which was then broken into pieces and installed in a huge studio tank along with the actors while electric blades churned up the water to simulate rough seas.

Golitzen was helped considerably on *Foreign Correspondent* by the venerable William Cameron Menzies, who is credited with "special production effects," but whose wit and sense of scale flash all over the film. The intricate scene involving the trundles and gears that turn inside the windmill as McCrea tries to overhear the conspirators and rescue their kidnapped victim recalls Menzies's own designs for *Things to Come* (1936), turned on their head by Hitchcock to suggest danger instead of progress. Likewise, Hitchcock's use of dramatic lighting to illuminate different parts of the interior of the windmill in all probability owes much to Menzies's sensibility, plus the expert technique of veteran cinematographer Rudolf Maté.

Throughout his career, windows played an important role in Hitchcock's design schemes (even turning into the subject of one film, as we shall see). In *Foreign Correspondent*, Golitzen's sets are filled with windows, from the porthole windows that greet McCrea on his first voyage to London, to the bay windows in the Savoy Hotel where McCrea meets Day and Marshall for the first time, to the windows of the windmill. The windows are there to tempt the hero to freedom, or to provide a means of escape. McCrea escapes through a window three times in *Foreign Correspondent:* first from the windmill, then from the hotel (where, in a comical aside, he knocks out two of the letters of the hotel's neon sign so that it reads "HOT EUROPE"), and finally from the drowned airplane.

Perhaps then it is no coincidence that McCrea's famous final speech, in which he exhorts America to "keep those lights burning" as the darkness of war crosses England, is delivered in a radio studio designed with floor-to-ceiling windows. We watch the terrified citizenry scatter as the bombs begin to fall and the real world that we have only tantalizingly glimpsed through the windows comes literally crashing in. McCrea's plea was Hitchcock's—and Hitchcock's was the nation's—as the specter of another war covered the world.

SHADOW OF A DOUBT

Alfred Hitchcock's mother died just before production began on *Shadow of a Doubt* (1943). This, combined with the war in Europe, left Hitchcock feeling physically and spiritually marooned. As a result, *Shadow of a Doubt* is one of Hitchcock's subtlest and most personal films. The elements of intrigue, romance, suspicion, and murder are present, but the setting—small-town America—and characters—a young girl on the verge of becoming a woman and her favorite uncle—are less stereotypical and consequently more complex than usual.

The art director on *Shadow of a Doubt* was Robert Boyle, working under the current supervisory art director at Universal, John B. Goodman. Hitchcock couldn't be said to have had a favorite art director, but he worked with Boyle more often than with any other designer. Boyle designed all or part of five films for Hitchcock: *Saboteur* (1942), *Shadow of a Doubt*, *North by Northwest* (1959), *The Birds* (1963), and *Marnie* (1964). Always unstinting in his praise of the master director, he was quoted by Donald Spoto as saying that Hitchcock was "one of the few who

really knows the materials of his craft and their effect."

Shadow of a Doubt differs from most other Hitchcock films in that it was shot almost entirely on location in Santa Rosa, California. Every detail, from the soda shops and touring cars to the verdant splendor of the tree-lined suburban streets, is authentic and reassuring—and all the more terrifying, then, when young Charlie (Teresa Wright) discovers a homicidal maniac among them in the person of her once-adored Uncle Charlie (Joseph Cotten). The Newtons are supposed to be "a representative American family" and everyone in the town knows young Charlie by name. Even the set decoration in the Newton home is deliberately—perhaps satirically—vintage Americana. Floral wallpaper, ceramic animals, white gauze curtains, solid oak chairs and sideboards, curio cabinets, a Frigidaire, and a tea table fill every space in the home.

Slowly, as if by insinuation, the bright sparkle of Santa Rosa gets replaced by something darker and more sinister, just as young Charlie's idyllic, adolescent view of life becomes poisoned by the reality of her uncle's situation. When Charlie goes to the library at night and discovers the horrible truth, the camera pulls back to reveal the girl and her monstrous shadow alone in the huge, empty room. Later Uncle Charlie chases her down the streets of Santa Rosa, and the crowds are no longer friendly but threatening. The two of them go into a

Shadow of a Doubt (1943)

Downtown Santa Rosa, California, with typical Hitchcockian irony: the funeral of a hero who is really a murderer. (Universal)

smoke-filled bar, which represents the very antithesis of small-town American life. "I've never been in a place like this," young Charlie protests, to which her uncle replies, "You're just an ordinary little girl . . . and I brought you nightmares." By the end of the film, the inversion of light and good with dark and evil is nearly complete. The night before Uncle Charlie is planning to leave town, the two Charlies end up on the dark porch staircase, the girl basking in incandescent light, the man in total darkness. As young Charlie moves out of the light and into the black, she says: "Go away or I'll kill you myself."

The final shot of the film—of Uncle Charlie's funeral procession through downtown Santa Rosa—is a marvelous example of how Boyle's art direction fits into Hitchcock's sensibility. The townsfolk think Uncle Charlie was a noble citizen and mourn him; they do not know that he died trying to toss his niece from a moving train. This cheerful facade of a small-town American main street is a sham. Boyle has expressed the soul of the movie with the simplest of devices: a real street. It's a stage, but not a set. True to Hitchcock, nothing is as it appears to be.

REAR WINDOW

In *Rear Window* (1954), windows are not only part of the design scheme but the subject of the film. L. B. Jeffries (James Stewart), an internationally renowned news photographer, is confined to his Greenwich Village apartment due to a broken leg received in the line of duty. To relieve his boredom, he begins to watch his neighbors through his rear window, at first passively, then intently with binoculars and a telescopic lens as he suspects one of his neighbors of murder.

Rear Window is one of Alfred Hitchcock's "trick" movies. Along with *Lifeboat* (1944) and *Rope, Rear Window* has only one set. For such a conceit to succeed, the set must be initially interesting and the subsequent direction must be clever, creative, and dramatic. On all counts, *Rear Window* triumphs, eclipsing the earlier experiments with its compelling, multidimensional story and most of all with its extraordinarily complex set— over thirty apartments built fully to scale and a dozen of them individually decorated according to the whims of their fictional tenants.

The set for *Rear Window* was designed by the great Hal Pereira, then supervisory art director for Paramount, and Joseph McMillan Johnson, with the usual contributions from Hitchcock himself. It was probably Hitchcock (in association with his screenwriter, John Michael Hayes) who dreamed up the apartment complex and its layout. It was up to Pereira and Johnson, and expert Paramount set decorators Sam Comer and Ray Mayer, to make the set look familiar and threatening at the same time. Ironically, this "one set" was the biggest ever built on the Paramount lot. Here we find a composer, whose apartment is quite logically centered around his grand piano; a snooping sculptress; a man who raises the blinds for a breath of fresh air away from his new bride; "Miss Torso," a voluptuous blonde dancer; "Miss Lonelyhearts," who sets up romantic dinners for two at which she is the only guest; and ominously, a burly jewelry salesman with an invalid, demanding wife.

Like saints, the lives of these characters are revealed through their attributes, doubling as set decorations. For instance, we learn that Jeffries is a news photographer in the first shot of the film. After the credits, the camera pans across the courtyard of rear windows, into Jeffries's apartment, to his face, his broken leg, a smashed camera, and a news photograph of a racecar crash. Then it flies out the window once more for a more leisurely trip around the courtyard, where we meet the sculptress with her work, Miss Torso stretching, the salesman with his cases, Miss Lonelyhearts at housework, and so on. This sequence, consisting of a slow, circular pan from right to left and then reversed from left to right, is the visual motif that anchors the movie—it is the sum of the known universe according to the film (except for a small slice of the street visible through an alley). What Jeffries does is thus by implication what we do by watching him. His nurse, Stella (Thelma Ritter), puts it more succinctly, "We've become a race of Peeping Toms."

Rear Window is about voyeurism. It is not coincidental that the shape of the windows of the apartments that Jeffries spies upon are nearly the same size and shape as movie screens—he's watching his movie, we're watching ours. His motivations are similar to ours, as well. He has a deeply unsatisfying, intimate conversation with his girlfriend, Lisa (Grace Kelly). After she leaves, he immediately resumes his scanning, as if it relieved his frustration to substitute the turmoil of other people's lives for his own, just as movies provide a fantasy world when one needs to escape from the pressures of everyday life.

The props and set decorations in *Rear Window* continually contribute to the escalating sense of voyeurism. First Jeffries asks Lisa to fetch his binoculars, then his telescopic lens. As he circles around the windows of the apartments, the editing pace picks up and the blackouts between scenes occur more frequently, providing visual clues that underline Jeffries's increasing nervousness. The shades that could effectively end Jeffries's movie (and ours) finally come down about twenty minutes before the end, but almost immediately a scream rings out in the courtyard. One couple's dog is dead, and everyone's movie screen pops into action once more. Lisa goes over to the suspect's apartment, where of course she gets trapped and is very nearly assaulted. Jeffries is no more free to help while watching her than we are. When the killer finds out Jeffries has been watching him, he comes over to commit another murder. Jeffries is alone and trapped in his hospital chair, just as we are trapped in our cinema seat, helpless. The conceit is simple, elegant, and perfect.

Rear Window ends with another slow, circular pan shot like the one that began it, showing the happy endings of the lives of the other apartment dwellers and concluding in Jeffries's place. Having survived falling from his window, he now has both legs in a cast. Lisa is shown reading a book on the Himalayas, implying that she has consented to join him on his next business trip. But she's holding onto an issue of *Bazaar* magazine, just in case—a sly and altogether typical Hitchcock ending.

NORTH BY NORTHWEST

North by Northwest (1959) is Alfred Hitchcock on a grand scale—a terrifying action and adventure story, a witty and adult romance, and a dazzling visual travelogue all rolled up into one. That *North by Northwest* has such attractive production values should come as no surprise—it was Hitchcock's only film for MGM, the studio whose name had become synonymous with glamour, even in its dotage. *North by Northwest* also features two of the studio's greatest art directors, Merrill Pye and

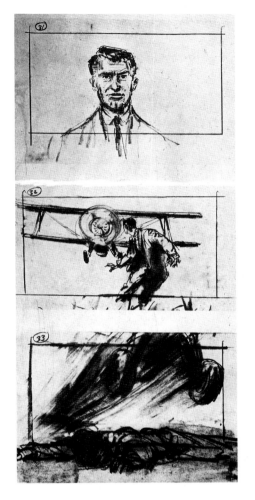

TOP: *North by Northwest* (1959)

A sheet of sketches for the famous crop-duster sequence. (MGM)

ABOVE: *North by Northwest*

Roger Thornhill (Cary Grant) amid the claustrophobia-inducing corn. (MGM)

LEFT: North by Northwest

The Department of the Interior wouldn't let Alfred Hitchcock go to Mount Rushmore, so he built a scale model of the national monument in the studio. He probably preferred it this way. (MGM)

INSET: North by Northwest

Cary Grant grabs a cigarette during a quiet moment on the slopes of Mount Rushmore. (MGM)

North by Northwest

Eve Kendall (Eva Marie Saint) con-
fronts Roger Thornhill (Cary Grant)
and Phillip Van Damm (James
Mason) in the cafeteria at Mount
Rushmore. (MGM)

OPPOSITE:
North by Northwest

A sketch of Roger Thornhill on the
ledge of the Van Damm house. (MGM)

William A. Horning, working in this case for Robert
Boyle, Hitchcock's trusted right-hand design man.

Merrill Pye had been a favored art director at MGM
for nearly thirty years; among his more notable credits
are *Babes in Arms* (1939) and *Ziegfeld Follies* (1945).
Horning, of course, worked on *The Wizard of Oz* (1939)
and was assigned to the studio's *Ben-Hur* (1959) simultaneously with *North by Northwest,* as was special-
effects master A. Arnold Gillespie. (How both men did
double-duty for such demanding directors as Hitchcock
and William Wyler challenges the imagination.) Boyle
supervised all three men and their crews; this was
almost certainly Hitchcock's call, since Hitchcock knew
Boyle well and had worked with him before. After all,
Hitchcock had already storyboarded the entire film and
probably only wanted someone in charge who could turn
his storyboards into full-scale sets with a minimal
amount of interference from the art department.

North by Northwest tells the story of a Manhattan
advertising executive, Roger Thornhill (Cary Grant),

who is mistaken for a federal agent and kidnapped, framed, and chased from the United Nations to Chicago to Mount Rushmore. The sets, in glorious Technicolor, are resolutely modern, concentrating on the glass towers of midtown New York and the United Nations, the functional interiors of the Twentieth Century Limited train and the Ambassador East hotel, and the touristy Americana of Mount Rushmore National Park. Equally modern are the links from location to location, usually the nondescript interiors of large touring cars or taxicabs, occasionally a train or even a mundane bus. The colors are alternately pastel or jazzy, like most fifties decor, from the ocher overtones of the New York hotel suite to the icy blues and red leather of the Intelligence Agency office, to the sand, lime, faded pink, and powder blue palette of the Twentieth Century's dining car. The elegant designs and relaxing colors reassure us of the security and familiarity of this world—undermined, of course, when in their midst violence strikes and logic falls apart.

Although always engaging, the settings for *North by Northwest* are particularly brilliant in three scenes: the attack in the cornfield, the rescue at the Van Damm house, and the chase on Mount Rushmore. In the famous cornfield sequence, Thornhill is attacked in the middle of a flat field by a crop duster determined to run him down or poison him with DDT. This is the quintessential Hitchcock set: nothing. The field is endless, flat, and brown,

except where there is corn—there it is endless, flat, and gold. The sky, a huge expanse of blue, seems to crush the earth. The irony—an attack in this huge, abandoned space after an easy escape in the much more perilous confines of the train compartment—is pure Hitchcock, and the design, completely artless, is probably Hitchcock's own.

The Van Damm house, nestled into the side of one of the Black Mountains, is a Frank Lloyd Wright nightmare that underscores the art direction's intense modern tone. Half the house dangles dangerously over a cliff, supported by metal beams. The floor-to-ceiling windows facing all sides are Hitchcock's own way of telling us that there is a lot to be revealed. In this scene, Thornhill comes to rescue Eve Kendall (Eva Marie Saint), the double agent with whom he's fallen in love. As Thornhill climbs along the arched angles of the metal beams and claws his way up the rough-hewn stone walls, he's like a modern Daedalus making his way through a Usonian labyrinth in search of that last layer of truth that Hitchcock always cunningly conceals.

North by Northwest ends with the famous chase across the presidential faces of Mount Rushmore. Of course, the actors weren't really imperiling their lives by battling with their fists atop one of the nation's most treasured icons. The Department of the Interior revoked the production's permit for use of the monument when Hitchcock boasted of running his cast all over it, but Hitchcock was probably gunning for publicity. The only time the actual monument appears in the film is in a long shot taken from the National Park cafeteria. The remainder of the sequence was filmed in Los Angeles with scale-model plaster casts designed by Boyle.

The scene concludes with Thornhill pulling the desperate Eve up the mountainside from her death and—through a clever edit—landing her in his berth on the Twentieth Century. The train then zooms into a tunnel, a cute bit of imagery that has titillated audiences ever since. In a film full of monumental buildings and built monuments, this is Hitchcock's final tribute to the triumph of man over stone.

THE SLOW PULL OF FATE: RICHARD DAY AND REALISM

Richard Day is one of the unsung heroes of Hollywood. His influence on the visual language of the motion picture industry as it matured in the years before and after World War II is unparalleled. Other art directors may have been more powerful—Cedric Gibbons at MGM—and others more talented—Hans Dreier and Hal Pereira at Paramount had a more highly developed sense of aesthetics—but Day transformed the staginess of a standing set into something more elusive and profound: the setting as character. In a film designed by Day, the background and settings always seem to flow from the principal characters' individual sense of the world, and their actions within this world are thus as proscribed as if it were the real one.

Day broke into the business by painting sets in the silent era. His talent was quickly recognized, and by the early twenties he had landed the plum position of chief set designer for Erich von Stroheim. His monumental casino for *Greed* (1924) and glittering ballrooms for *The Merry Widow* (1925) are legendary and did much to promote von Stroheim's reputation as a hedonist and spendthrift, but they are not truly representative of Day's work. His major achievements came later, when he worked with independent producer Samuel Goldwyn. Like von Stroheim, Goldwyn had enough taste and money to pro-

Dead End (1937) *For the film, Richard Day expanded Norman Bel Geddes's original Broadway set, adding to it a* *... (Goldwyn/United Artists)*

duce prestigious films and just the right amount of show-
manship to know how to dazzle an audience. Day and
Goldwyn clicked because they both believed Hollywood
could handle more realism—hard-hitting stories of crime
and city life, as well as personal stories of bittersweet
romance.

Day's brand of realism is different from that of Warner Brothers. Jack L. Warner was constantly running out
of money, and the shabbiness of the company's sets was
eloquent but somewhat inadvertent. Working with Goldwyn, Day always had enough money. The goal was not to
pound down the Hollywood gloss but to gently part it, so
that the talent of the actors would shine through and the
settings would naturally surround them. Because Day's
sets so carefully modulate the space between uncompromising realism and show-business slickness, their appeal
is universal and long lasting. In their way, his sets helped
Hollywood make the transition from the escapism and
innocence of screwball comedies and love stories to the
more adult themes that have become the staple today.
From the comfortable settings that underscore the
uncomfortable lives in *Dodsworth,* to the self-contained,
rotten universe of *Dead End,* to the deadening yet
hopeful streets in *On the Waterfront,* Richard Day was a
beacon who lighted the direction of production design in
Hollywood for almost thirty years.

DODSWORTH

Dodsworth (1936), based on Sinclair Lewis's novel and
Sidney Howard's play, tells the story of a middle-aged
married couple, Samuel and Fran Dodsworth (Walter
Huston and Ruth Chatterton), and the changes that
overwhelm them when Sam retires and they sail for an
extended vacation in Europe. Fran, fearing old age, foolishly flings herself at younger men, while Sam, at first
tolerant, later rebels and eventually leaves his wife for a
more sympathetic widow, Edith Cortright (Mary Astor).
These very painful yet truthful revelations come in a
series of dramatic confrontations set amid the simple
elegance of the Dodsworths' station in life: their white-
pillared mansion in Zenith, Indiana; the stateroom of the
Queen Mary; first-class hotel rooms in Paris and Rome;
and a lakeside villa near Naples.

For each of these settings, Richard Day designed an

TOP: *Dodsworth* (1936)

*Samuel Dodsworth (Walter Huston) bids farewell to
the company he created. In the finished film, the
sign outside the office window reads "Dodsworth,"
not "Union Motors." (Goldwyn/United Artists)*

ABOVE: *Dodsworth*

*Lockert (David Niven) flirts with Fran Dodsworth
(Ruth Chatterton) in her steamship cabin. (Gold-
wyn/United Artists)*

TOP: *Dodsworth*

Samuel Dodsworth (Walter Huston) and his wife, Fran (Ruth Chatterton), in Paris, courtesy of Richard Day's refined hotel suite and a trick photograph placed outside the false window. (Goldwyn/United Artists)

ABOVE: *Dodsworth*

Gone are the straight lines of the factory and the stuffy phoniness of Paris: Samuel Dodsworth (Walter Huston) and Edith Cortright (Mary Astor) amid the soft lines and earthy decor of Mrs. Cortright's Italian villa. (Goldwyn/United Artists)

elegant, unified space that surrounds each character, helping to define him or her and providing the audience with a visual context for the characters' internal struggles. At their home in Zenith, the piles of art, pillared halls, and parquet floors—once symbols of Sam's success, quickly turn into a suffocating trap, first for Fran and eventually for Sam as well. The *Queen Mary,* with its tantalizing view of the ocean and freedom visible through the porthole window of their stateroom, is similarly comfortable and threatening. By the end of the film, the lead characters' roles are reversed. Fran sits in the midst of the stuffy elegance of her Viennese hotel room, surrounded by the heavy draperies, dark wood furnishings, and gilt fleur-de-lis wallpaper, watching the snow fall outside her window. Meanwhile, Sam and Edith are lounging by the fountain in their flagstone-paved garden in Italy, exposed to and accepting of nature.

In a film based on a literary source such as *Dodsworth,* one would expect a certain amount of symbolism in the decor, but what makes Day's set designs more than symbols is their inordinate naturalness and simplicity. Day has perfected the art of making a statement without saying anything, one definition of great art direction. The Indiana home, the Parisian hotel room, the villa by the lake were all chosen by Sam because that's where he felt he needed to be at the time, just as the Vienna hotel room was chosen by Fran. The divergence of their final choices tells us as much about their incompatibility as their words. At the end of the film, each crosses a body of water to conclude a personal journey. For Fran, it is the Atlantic Ocean and home to an uncertain future. For Sam, it is the Bay of Naples and freedom.

DEAD END

Like *Dodsworth, Dead End* (1937) was based on a play, in this case a very successful one by Sidney Kingsley. Also like *Dodsworth, Dead End* was directed by the great William Wyler. In *Dead End,* the master director turned his attention away from the troubled lives of the middle-aged rich to the more perilously troubled lives of the young and the poor. It is a relentlessly downbeat drama, despite its supposedly happy ending (the gangster is dead and the poor but happy couple are reunited).

Richard Day's work on *Dead End* consists of one set, the street implied in the title and the pier on which it ends, with rows of small shops and tenements jammed on one side of the street and the backside of a high-class apartment building on the other—an expanded version of Norman Bel Geddes's stage set. The film opens with a shot of the New York skyline and pans down past the skyscrapers, skimming over the rooftops and clothes-lines until it comes to a halt at the end of the street and the edge of the dirty river. This is where we stay for the rest of the film, until the last shot, when the camera repeats the movement in reverse. Clearly the street is meant to be seen as another character in the story—perhaps even the main character with the opening and closing "lines."

The street set in *Dead End* is not so realistic that it dissolves into the film, nor is it Hollywood-stylized enough to break away from the characters. One telling incident that occurred during production underscores this ambivalence. It seems that Samuel Goldwyn didn't care much for realistic-looking sets (he nixed Wyler's suggestion to shoot the entire film on the streets of New York). Every morning during the filming of *Dead End,* he would wander down onto the set and pick up the pieces of artfully strewn garbage that Day, Wyler, and property man Irving Sandler had put there. Despite Goldwyn's efforts, however, a few bits of startling realism stayed in. The interior of Tommy and Drina's apartment is so close and stuffed with pots, pans, bedclothes, cleaning tools, and knickknacks that the narrow space of the street seems comfortable in comparison. On the other hand, the dock and pier where the Dead End kids cavort resemble a low-class nightclub stage, arranged in tiers so the actors could all be easily seen.

Day's work on *Dead End* is more or less glimpsed in its entirety in the first two minutes of the film. From then on it was up to cinematographer Gregg Toland to

enhance the setting and reveal its subtleties. Toland's famous "deep focus" camera work allows the audience to glimpse passersby puttering around in the darkest recesses of the set: workers making deliveries, children playing on a stoop, cars driving by. This increases the illusion of reality by adding another dimension to the stage-bound nature of the single set. Additionally, Toland often points his camera down to the gutter or up to the high-rise to emphasize the physical as well as the social differences between the two classes.

The set looks its best during the climactic chase between Baby Face Martin (Humphrey Bogart) and Dave (Joel McCrea). Toland, Wyler, and editor Daniel Mandell utilize every aspect of the set like a writer uses words. The men pass through a dark alley, into a smoke-filled basement, up again to the street, and then to the roof by means of the fire escape. When the bullets fly, Bogart comes crashing back down to the alley. This tightly edited sequence of images sums up the meaning of the film by intertwining the poverty of the characters' lives and the inevitability of death. Classic Toland, classic Day, and extremely forward looking in its uncompromising realism.

Dead End, however, does not end with this tragedy but with the Dead End kids gamboling on the street set, the remaining cast assembled more or less for their final bow. The effect is slightly uplifting, somewhat stylized, and satisfying in the conventional sense of the word. Yet deep down inside, it is clear that at least one of these kids will be in trouble again soon, and though the audience can rise up with the camera over the rooftops and tall buildings, the kids most probably can't.

ON THE WATERFRONT

In 1939 Richard Day ended his association with Samuel Goldwyn and went to work for Darryl F. Zanuck at 20th Century–Fox. Day was at his best when working with strong directors, and Zanuck provided them for him, most especially John Ford, with whom Day worked on *How Green Was My Valley* and *Tobacco Road* (both 1941). But Hollywood was changing, and after the war Day again struck out on his own, both as a means of self-protection against a crumbling industry and to have the chance to work on the kinds of productions that inter-

Dead End

William Wyler (seated) directing Humphrey Bogart and Marjorie Main (on the fire escape). (Goldwyn/United Artists)

On the Waterfront (1954)

Terry Malloy (Marlon Brando) and Edie Doyle (Eva Marie Saint) run for their lives. The alley is real. (Columbia)

ested him, films that dealt with contemporary problems in a realistic setting. His first foray into this territory, *Edge of Doom* (1950), directed by Mark Robson with Charles Vidor, was a mediocre drama about a wayward youth. But then Day met Elia Kazan. The two films that Day designed for Kazan, *A Streetcar Named Desire* (1951) and *On the Waterfront* (1954), were groundbreaking in many ways. Finally, controversial subjects were faced head-on, ordinary people's lives were not glamorized, and happy endings were not guaranteed. For *Streetcar,* Day's assignment was to create one set based on a play, much as he did in *Dead End.* But for *Waterfront,* the ground rules shifted considerably.

Budd Schulberg's screenplay about a corrupt waterfront union and its effect on the lives of poor longshoremen cried out for a realistic visual treatment, and Day and Kazan delivered: the entire film, with the exception of a few short interior sequences, was shot on location in Hoboken, New Jersey, among the very workers whose lives it was trying to portray. *On the Waterfront* was not the first major Hollywood production to be filmed on location, but it was the most successful one to date, and it helped to kill the studio-based art departments forever. From this moment on, the fantasy world of the studio belonged to musicals (a dying genre) and filmed plays; everything else went outdoors.

Much of the visual effect of the locations in *On the Waterfront* comes from the perfect integration of the actors and the screenplay with the settings. The Actors Studio, a prominent school for young American performers formed by Kazan and others in the late forties, was doing the same thing for acting that location shooting was doing for film settings: making it look more real. Much of the cast of *On the Waterfront,* including all the stars—Marlon Brando, Eva Marie Saint, and Karl Malden—were at one time or another members of the Actors Studio. Schulberg's screenplay was not based on a novel or a play, as was usually the case, but on a series of newspaper articles by Malcolm Johnson. Thus prepared, Day's job was simple. All he really had to do was make sure his "found sets" would come across undistorted on the screen.

The opening shot of the dock, with the covered storage bay on the left, the union's "shack" in the center, and a tugboat shimmying on the river's surface on the right, is a complete portrait of the milieu of the film. The heart of *On the Waterfront* is this dock: the film begins and ends here. Throughout the film the exteriors are all gray, either from the perpetual rain and cold or from the light being shut out by the freighters and derricks that line the shore. The interiors are either smoke-filled and dark, like Johnny Friendly's bar, or plain and cheap, like the bare brick walls of the church basement or the peeling wallpaper in Edie's railroad flat. Most evocative is the scene where Edie Doyle (Eva Marie Saint) and Father Barry (Karl Malden) walk out of the church, through a park shrouded in mist, and then along the river in front of an iron fence that reveals a sooty, gray Manhattan skyline behind them. This exactly parallels a scene in the Italian neorealist drama *Rome, Open City* (1945), in which an unmarried and pregnant Anna Magnani asks her priest for help while walking along a similar fence and cityscape in Rome. In this scene, *On the Waterfront* announced itself as the first American neorealist masterpiece.

On the Waterfront is also a story of sinfulness and redemption. Day fills the screen with visual references that emphasize religious themes. Some are obvious, like the rock that flies through the window of the church or the scene where Father Barry is transported to "heaven" on the flatbed of a dockside loading bay. But there are other, subtle images that reinforce the conceit of the world as a church. The roof where Terry Malloy (Marlon Brando) goes to get a little bit of relief from his life is a forest of cruciform antennae; his pigeon coops are his church, as much as the docks are Father Barry's. Both the church and the Irish pub where Terry and Edie go to have a beer have stained-glass windows, linking them visually. And most dramatically, in the film's final scene, when Terry rises up from his beating and leads the men back to work, he is the resurrected Christ and the dock is his Jerusalem.

Ironically, much of the location work in *On the Waterfront* resembles the silent-film classics of thirty years earlier—the primitiveness of the settings, once unfortunate but necessary, had now become deliberate and desirable. The industry had come full circle, and Day, who did so much with Erich von Stroheim to elevate Hollywood film sets to new heights in *Greed,* now found himself lionized for taking them to new lows. Many scenes in *On the Waterfront,* such as Father Barry's ascent from the "hole" or Terry breaking into Edie's flat and forcing himself upon her, are virtually silent, save for Leonard Bernstein's score, and depend on Day's resourcefulness and simplicity for much of their emotional impact. Day won his sixth Academy Award (alone or shared) for *On the Waterfront,* more than any other art director in Hollywood history except Cedric Gibbons.

Richard Day worked in Hollywood right up to his death in 1972; his next-to-last film was the overblown but unforgettable *Tora! Tora! Tora!* (1970). Day spent fifty years in the business; the nearly two hundred films that he partly or completely designed provide overwhelming evidence of his versatility, creativeness, and professionalism. If Day's career needed to be summed up, one would have to look no further than *Dodsworth, Dead End,* or *On the Waterfront* to see what he did: he widened the definition of realism in Hollywood. In short, he made movies look more real.

TWO COLOR MASTERPIECES: MARY POPPINS AND GONE WITH THE WIND

In these days of shoebox-size theaters and home video, it is hard to imagine the experience of watching a movie on a 60-foot silver screen. The luckiest ones have their memories; the rest of us must learn of it vicariously, lapping up descriptions of the old movie palaces from books and documentaries. While it is true that the cinema is a collaborative art, requiring the cooperation of technicians, writers, actors, musicians, and executives alike, it is still primarily a visual one. What is seen on the screen—and how it is seen—is the memory most strongly retained long after the name of the producer or screenwriter is forgotten.

The heyday of Hollywood's influence on American popular culture and the era of the movie palace was simultaneous with the popularity of Technicolor, the most famous color-film process. This relationship is not coincidental. Technicolor re-creates the world as a magical place; its complex cameras and dye-based printing turn natural colors into something just a bit brighter, richer, and more intense, in the same way that the big screen provided moviegoers with love stories and adventures that were larger than life. The first three-strip (full-spectrum) Technicolor feature was *Becky Sharp* (1935); by the mid-fifties, thanks to a newer and more naturalistic color stock developed by Eastman Kodak, Technicolor became obsolete.

Gone with the Wind (1939) *Atlanta (now at full scale) under siege. (MGM)*

During Technicolor's reign, Hollywood had the biggest attendance figures (proportionally) in its history. Hollywood was America, and Technicolor was Hollywood.

Gone with the Wind (1939) and *Mary Poppins* (1964) are bookends to this era. The former is perhaps the greatest color film ever made, filled with the newness of the color universe—long, bold, and overwhelming in its ambition. The latter seems in retrospect to be candy-colored Hollywood's last gasp, with its nursery-rhyme score, child's viewpoint, and coloring-book aura. For once the time-honored tradition of "in order of appearance" will be abandoned. We will begin with the end, so that we can end with the beginning.

MARY POPPINS

Walt Disney's *Mary Poppins* (1964) was the last family musical—at least until the company picked up the torch again with *The Little Mermaid* (1989) and *Beauty and the Beast* (1991). Its combination of animation, special effects, vaudeville humor, and instantly memorable songs has proven irresistible to several generations of children and adults alike. The magnificent art direction on *Mary Poppins* was supervised by Carroll Clark, the same man who, working for Van Nest Polglase thirty years earlier, created the dance sets for Fred Astaire and Ginger Rogers. Clark was assisted by William H. Tuntke, with set decoration by the great Paramount decorator Emile Kuri and Hal Gausman. In addition, *Mary Poppins* required the services of an animation art director, McLaren Stewart, as well as a special-effects team led by long-time Disney associate Peter Ellenshaw.

Their work shows effortlessly on the screen. The expected conflict between the live-action sequences and the animation never materializes; the animation backgrounds look very much like the painted backgrounds of London that open and close the picture during the supposedly "live" sequences, and the Technicolor of Cherry Tree Lane and the park is closer to the color of the animation than to reality. It stands to reason that if Bert (Dick Van Dyke), Mary Poppins (Julie Andrews), and the children can leap from one environment to the other, we should be able to do so as well. Clark's standard interiors, such as the Banks' house—with its green marble,

heavy drapes, deeply carved mantelpiece, and tabletops full of flowers and pottery—are routine but comfortable. *Mary Poppins*'s settings truly come to life in the film's most outrageous fantasy sequences: the walk in the park and the musical number "Feed the Birds."

As Mary and the children go to meet Bert in the park, the air is filled with a magical fog, covering the soft green and pink blossoms of the early London spring with mystery and suggesting the beginning of a magical adventure. Their adventure comes, as Mary shows Bert and the children how to jump into Bert's chalk drawings. For the next thirty minutes or so, the live cast prances about an animated tea party and country fair to the joyful sound of "Jolly Holiday." As the carousel horses at the fair break loose, the actors find themselves in the midst of an animated fox hunt. It is only when a thunderstorm threatens to destroy the chalk drawings and trap the actors forever that they feel the need to jump back to reality. The initial change from a caricatured Edwardian London to the cartoon country is so subtle and believable that it is almost startling to discover, when the rain comes and the drawings begin to melt on the screen, that this particular reality was any more fragile than the other.

Although much shorter, the "Feed the Birds" sequence is the lyrical heart of *Mary Poppins*. Mary tells the children about an old woman who sits on the steps of Saint Paul's Cathedral and asks for twopence for bags of peanuts to feed the hungry pigeons. The children are in their nursery, which is very blue (in the lighting and the wallpaper). Mary is wearing a blue frock, and Michael a pair of blue pajamas. As she sings "Feed the Birds," she picks up a snow globe of Saint Paul's and we see a flock of animated white pigeons inside it instead of snow. Still inside the globe, the Bird Lady (Jane Darwell) pathetically begs on behalf of her birds. With the deep blue shades of sorrow and night swirling around her in tandem with the white birds and the imposing painted background of the cathedral, the animated sequence built around the Bird Lady is one of the most purely bittersweet and emotional moments ever put on film, reaching for both sadness and hope at the same time. It is also purely cinematic, a fantasy within a fantasy, one of the Disney art department's finest achievements, and as well, the catalyst to the events in the city and at the bank the next day that finally unite the family in love and

Art director Carroll Clark, c. 1935.

free Mary to rescue another household.

Mary Poppins ends with the happy family all singing "Let's Go Fly a Kite," as Technicolor kites of red, yellow, and green sail merrily over the park. Meanwhile, Mary takes off with her umbrella, passing one last time over the pink blossoms of Cherry Tree Lane, up into the clouds above the painted backdrop of London, where the film began. It was never real, yet nothing has ever looked more real before or since.

GONE WITH THE WIND

When the subject of *Gone with the Wind* comes up—which it does regularly—the first persons most people think of are Scarlett O'Hara (Vivien Leigh) and Rhett Butler (Clark Gable). Perhaps, if pressed, the name of the producer, David O. Selznick, comes to mind. Some people, myopic to Hollywood, will think of Margaret Mitchell, the author of the novel upon which the film was based. But it is unlikely that anyone would offer the name of the one man perhaps most responsible for the visual beauty of the film, its production designer, William Cameron Menzies.

Like Orson Welles, Menzies was a prodigy whose scope and ambition overwhelmed the industry. Before he turned thirty, he had designed one masterpiece, *The Thief of Bagdad* (1924, with Anton Grot), still the greatest example of fantastic set design in film history. When he was barely forty, Menzies collaborated with H. G. Wells and Vincent Korda on *Things to Come* (1936), which he also directed. By the time Selznick said "Get Menzies!" he was ready for what would prove to be his greatest assignment.

TOP: *Gone with the Wind*

Production designer William Cameron Menzies reviewing sketches. (MGM)

MIDDLE: *Gone with the Wind*

William Cameron Menzies (left) and art director Lyle Wheeler amid a variety of their sketching staff's handiwork. (MGM)

RIGHT: *Gone with the Wind*

MGM studio artist Wilbur Kurtz in front of his rendering of Tara. (MGM)

Menzies began, as he always did, by blocking out the sets through a series of detailed watercolor sketches that showed the placement of the actors and the camera angles as well as the scenery. For *Gone with the Wind,* there were well over two thousand sketches, prepared by Menzies, Wilbur Kurtz, a historian Selznick hired to provide accurate details for the settings, and Joseph McMillan Johnson, Menzies's assistant, later to be a major art director in his own right. On a production where leadership changed with the weather, Menzies's sketches provided visual stability. As director George Cukor was fired and replaced by Victor Fleming, then for a while Sam Wood, as scripts were written, torn up, rewritten, filmed, and refilmed, Menzies stuck to it, focusing the production on his designs. It is partly because of Menzies's powerful personality and over-whelming talent that so much of *Gone with the Wind* is visually harmonious, considering the scatterbrained shooting schedule and constant battle with and inter-ference from the producer that the cast and crew had to tolerate.

Menzies also directed a portion of *Gone with the Wind* when Fleming was ill or no one else on the set knew exactly what would work best. By most accounts, Menzies directed the Atlanta hospital sequence, includ-ing the famous pull-back shot of the rows of wounded and dying Confederate soldiers. (This shot had to be taken from a rented construction crane, since the high-est boom in Hollywood went only 25 feet up and Menzies wanted 90. Also, half the bodies are stuffed dummies; there weren't enough extras in Hollywood to fill out the set.) Menzies also directed the wonderfully dark and evocative sequences of Scarlett's return to Tara through enemy lines, as she hid under a bridge in the rain and ran a gauntlet through Shantytown. He was responsible for the famous dramatic ending to part one, when Scar-lett gags on a carrot and exclaims, "As God is my wit-ness, I'll never be hungry again," while the camera pulls back to capture her silhouette, the wreck of Tara, and a menacing, blasted tree.

With Menzies's pull and ambition, he has managed to overshadow the film's art director, Lyle Wheeler. As the supervisory art director for 20th Century–Fox through-out the late forties and fifties, Wheeler was responsible for the excellent work of the art department in a variety of films, from the rustic *My Darling Clementine* (1946)

to the gemlike *The Robe* (1953). On *Gone with the Wind,* timing, budgeting, coordination, and quality work were of equal importance, and it would have been Wheeler's lot to supervise all of it. Wheeler was not even Selznick's first choice. When Cukor was scheduled to direct, Hobe Erwin was Cukor's art director. In addition to Wheeler, Selznick hired an interior designer, Joseph B. Platt, to decorate the homes.

Menzies's sense of scale and scope and Wheeler's precision and attention to detail are evident in every minute of *Gone with the Wind*'s epic two hundred and twenty minutes. The resounding interiors of Tara and Twelve Oaks are spacious and comfortable but modest when compared with the near-tasteless exuberance of the mansion in Atlanta, with its overly ornamented white and gold spaces. It is almost as if the naive simplicity that was the South before the war, and Scarlett before meeting Rhett, was embodied by Tara and reflected in Scarlett's mother's frugal tastes, whereas the gauche materialism of the new mansion is symbolic of the new South and the new Scarlett—brazen, vibrant, and just a bit of an arriviste. There's a certain element of less-than-subtle symbolism, too, in the settings for the siege and burning of Atlanta, as the once-prosperous storehouses that fed the folks at Tara and Twelve Oaks disappear beneath the conflagration of war.

Menzies's mastery of the grand stroke in no way diminishes Wheeler's incredible ability to focus on the telling detail. *Gone with the Wind* is filled with small visual moments that are as important to the design of the film and its emotional strength as the epic ones. There is the pathetic little Christmas at Twelve Oaks, when Ashley Wilkes (Leslie Howard) comes home from the war. The Christmas tree is a barren, 2-foot pine with a few strands of gold tinsel; the house is bathed in a fad-ing, golden glow that highlights the worn wallpaper. Out-side, through a window, we see cold rain falling on a bare tree branch. There is no clearer nor purer example in film history of foreshadowing. Another good small moment comes later in the film, after the war, when Tara has become a washed-out hulk. Her once solid colors are now faded to brown and gray. Baths are arranged by hanging old blankets on ropes. As an overly literal exam-ple of how the settings help to define character, Scarlett rips down a piece of an old green-brocade curtain to make herself a proper dress.

Besides the epic scale of the settings and the sumptuous period details, the art direction in *Gone with the Wind* is also one of the most dazzling displays of color cinematography ever seen. Part of the credit for this, of course, goes to the film's cinematographers—Lee Garmes (who was fired by Selznick about a third of the way through), Ernest Haller (who had never shot a film in color), and Ray Rennahan (who filmed all the scenes Menzies directed). Somewhere on the set were the usual Technicolor consultants, including Natalie Kalmus, the former wife of the cocreator of the process, and Wilfred M. Cline, Rennahan's associate. Cline and Rennahan, most probably in association with Kalmus and the Technicolor organization, were testing a new color-negative stock that was several times more sensitive than the old one. This too helped to give *Gone with the Wind* a distinct and unique coloration.

In *Gone with the Wind,* Menzies captured the spirit of the romantic old South and its inevitable destruction and brought it to fiery fruition on the screen. Indeed, fire is the central visual metaphor of the film, and the colors of fire are its predominant hue. The interior of Tara is powder blue, trimmed in gold, the hallways at Twelve Oaks pristine white. Even before the fire begins in Atlanta, the dust of the streets is strangely orange, and the land that raised so many generations of Wilkes is red. Red, too, is the carpet that frames Scarlett's collapse and Rhett's eventual departure. Scarlett's resolution at the end of part one comes in the visual form of a black silhouette against a burning orange sunset. Even the names Rhett and Scarlett sound like the names of burning colors. This symbolic and descriptive use of color can be credited to Menzies.

Gone with the Wind has come to mean too much to American popular culture to be easily recast as a piece of Hollywood product; it is too important a part of film history to be called a poetic tribute to William Cameron Menzies's talents as a production designer. Yet it is both, triumphantly. To separate the legend of *Gone with the Wind* as it appears on the screen from the technical expertise, spirit of cooperation, and sheer business sense that was needed to complete it is to divorce it from the world that it truly reflects, the golden age of Hollywood. And to celebrate *Gone with the Wind* without acknowledging Menzies's contributions is to cheat all of us out of an important part of its history.

TOP: *Gone with the Wind*

Lyle Wheeler holding a storyboard for the burning of Atlanta. (MGM)

ABOVE: *Gone with the Wind*

Lyle Wheeler and an unidentified woman with a model of Atlanta. (MGM)

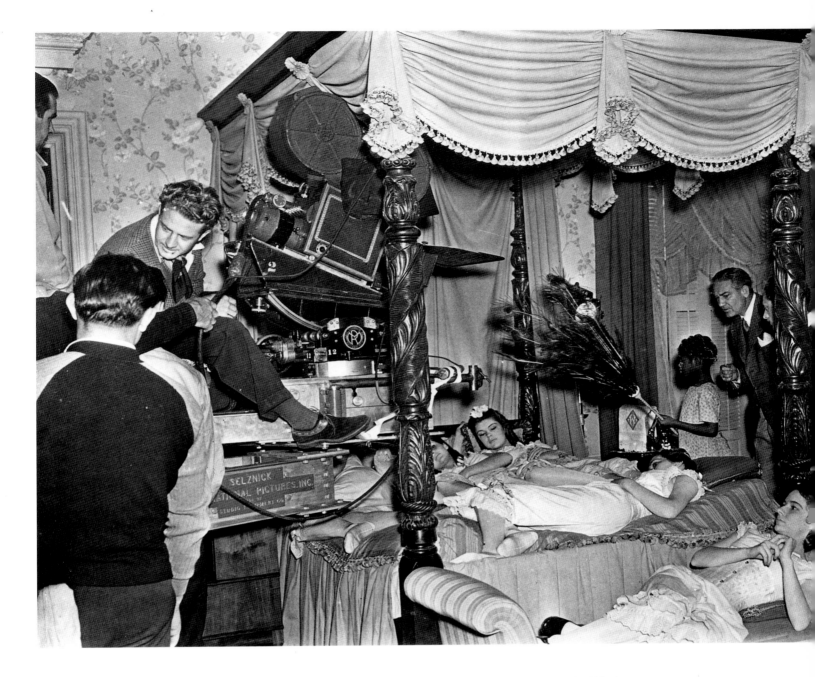

Gone with the Wind

Scarlett O'Hara (Vivien Leigh) and the girls take a nap under the watchful eyes of an MGM cameraman and director Victor Fleming (far right). (MGM)

BIBLIOGRAPHY

ARTICLES

Ballin, Hugo. "The Scenic Background." *Mentor* 9 (July 1921): 22–28.

Calhoun, John. "The Two Jakes." *Theatre Crafts* 24, no. 4 (April 1990): 31 ff.

Clark, Paul Sargent. "2001: A Design Preview." *Industrial Design* 15 (May 1968): 34–40.

Deutelbaum, Marshall. "Memory/Visual Design: The Remembered Sights of Blade Runner." *Literature-Film Quarterly* 17, no.1 (January 1989): 66.

Durgnat, Raymond. "Art for Film's Sake." *American Film* 7, no. 7 (May 1983): 41–45.

Fagan, Brian. "Digging DeMille." *Archaeology* 44, no. 2 (March/April 1981): 16–20.

Flint, Ralph. "Cedric Gibbons." *Creative Art* 11, no. 2 (October 1932): 117–19.

Kay, Jane Holtz. "When Hollywood Was Golden, The Movie Sets Were Too." *New York Times,* January 11, 1990.

"Ken Adam: Dialogue on Film." *American Film* 16, no. 2 (February 1991): 16–21.

Lachenbruch, Jerome. "Interior Decoration for the Movies: Studies from the Work of Cedric Gibbons and Gilbert White." *Arts & Decoration,* January 1921.

Mills, Bart. "The Brave New World of Production Design." *American Film* 7, no. 4 (January/February 1982): 40–43.

"Richard Sylbert: Dialogue on Film." *American Film* 11, no. 3 (December 1986): 12–16.

Rickey, Carrie. "Theatrical Realism." *Film Comment* 18, no. 1 (January/February 1982): 32–33.

Seebohm, Caroline. "Sweet Modesty." *Connoisseur,* July 1986: 33–37.

Silverthorne, Jeanne. "The Cave: Jeanne Silverthorne on Batman." *Artforum* 28, no. 1 (September 1989): 12–14.

Spiegel, Ellen. "Fred & Ginger Meet Van Nest Polglase." *The Velvet Light Trap,* no. 10 (1973).

Thomson, David. "The Art of the Art Director." *American Film* 2, no. 4 (February 1977): 12–20.

Troy, Carol. "Architect of Illusions (Film Production Designer Patrizia von Brandenstein)." *American Film* 15, no. 11 (August 1990): 32.

Verk, Stefen. "Designer for the Screen: Cedric Gibbons." *American Artist* 12, no. 9 (November 1948): 36–39, 68–69.

BOOKS

Adamson, Joe. *Groucho, Harpo, Chico, and Sometimes Zeppo: A History of the Marx Brothers.* New York: Simon and Schuster, 1973.

Albrecht, Donald. *Designing Dreams: Modern Architecture in the Movies.* New York: Harper & Row, 1986.

Anderegg, Michael A. *David Lean.* Boston: Twayne, 1984.

———. *William Wyler.* Boston: Twayne, 1979.

The Art of Hollywood: Fifty Years of Art Direction. London: Thames Television, 1979.

Balshofer, Fred J., and Arthur C. Miller. *One Reel a Week.* Berkeley: University of California Press, 1967.

Barsacq, Leon. *Caligari's Cabinet and Other Grand Illusions.* Boston: New York Graphic Society, 1976.

Baxter, John. *Hollywood in the Thirties.* New York: Barnes, 1968.

Berg, A. Scott. *Goldwyn: A Biography.* New York: Alfred A. Knopf, 1989.

Bergman, Andrew. *We're in the Money.* New York: New York University Press, 1971.

Bordwell, David, Janet Staiger, and Kristin Thompson. *The Classical Hollywood Cinema: Film Style and Mode of Production to 1960.* New York: Columbia University Press, 1985.

Brownlow, Kevin. *The Parade's Gone By.* New York: Alfred A. Knopf, 1968.

Capra, Frank. *The Name Above the Title.* New York: Macmillan, 1971.

Carey, Gary. *All the Stars in Heaven.* New York: Dutton, 1981.

Carringer, Robert. *The Making of Citizen Kane.* Berkeley: University of California Press, 1985.

Christie, Ian. *Arrows of Desire: The Films of Michael Powell and Emeric Pressburger.* London: Waterstone, 1985.

Clarens, Carlo. *An Illustrated History of the Horror Film.* New York: Putnam, 1967.

Coppola, Eleanor. *Notes.* New York: Simon and Schuster, 1979.

Croce, Arlene. *The Fred Astaire/Ginger Rogers Book.* New York: Outerbridge & Lazard, 1972.

Dettman, Bruce, and Michael Bedford. *The Horror Factory.* New York: Gordon Press, 1976.

Dick, Bernard F. *Billy Wilder.* Boston: Twayne, 1980.

Eisner, Lotte. *Fritz Lang.* New York: Oxford University Press, 1977.

Fitzgerald, Michael G. *Universal Pictures: A Panoramic History.* New Rochelle, N.Y.: Arlington House, 1977.

Fordin, Hugh. *The Movies' Greatest Musicals.* New York: Ungar, 1975.

Francisco, Charles. *You Must Remember This: The Filming of Casablanca.* Englewood Cliffs, N.J.: Prentice-Hall, 1980.

Fraser, George MacDonald. *The Hollywood History of the World.* London: M. Joseph, 1988.

Fricke, John, et al. *The Wizard of Oz: The Official 50th Anniversary Pictorial History.* New York: Warner Books, 1989.

Gallagher, Tag. *John Ford: The Man and His Films.* Berkeley: University of California Press, 1986.

Harmetz, Aljean. *The Making of the Wizard of Oz.* New York: Alfred A. Knopf, 1977.

Heisner, Beverly. *Hollywood Art: Art Direction in the Days of the Great Studios.* Jefferson, N.C.: McFarland, 1990.

Henderson, Robert. *D. W. Griffith: His Life and Work.* New York: Oxford University Press, 1972.

Hirschhorn, Clive. *The Universal Story.* London: Octopus, 1983.

Hollywood and History: Costume Design in Film. London: Thames and Hudson, 1987.

Jensen, Paul M. *The Cinema of Fritz Lang.* New York: Barnes, 1969.

Knox, Donald. *The Magic Factory: How MGM Made An American in Paris.* New York: Praeger, 1973.

Korda, Michael. *Charmed Lives.* New York: Random House, 1979.

Koszarski, Richard. *An Evening's Entertainment.* New York: Scribner, 1990.

Kulik, Karol. *Alexander Korda: The Man Who Could Work Miracles.* London: Allen, 1975.

Lambert, Gavin. *GWTW: The Making of Gone with the Wind.* Boston: Little, Brown, 1973.

Lasky, Betty. *RKO: The Biggest Little Major of Them All.* Englewood Cliffs, N.J.: Prentice-Hall, 1974.

Macgowan, Kenneth. *Behind the Screen: The History and Technique of Motion Pictures.* New York: Dell, 1965.

Madsen, Axel. *Billy Wilder.* London: Secker & Warburg, 1968.

Mandelbaum, Howard. *Forties Screen Style.* New York: St. Martin's Press, 1989.

Mathews, Jack. *The Battle of Brazil.* New York: Crown, 1987.

Matzek, Richard A. *Directory of Archival Collections on the History of Film in the United States.* Association of College and Research Libraries, 1983.

Mordden, Ethan. *The Hollywood Studios: House Style in the Golden Age of the Movies.* New York: Alfred A. Knopf, 1988.

Moss, Robert F. *The Films of Carol Reed.* New York: Columbia University Press, 1987.

Powell, Michael. *A Life in Movies.* New York: Alfred A. Knopf, 1987.

Salt, Barry. *Film Style and Technology: History and Analysis.* London: Starword, 1983.

Schatz, Thomas. *The Genius of the System.* New York: Pantheon, 1988.

Schickel, Richard. *D. W. Griffith: An American Life.* New York: Simon and Schuster, 1984.

Sennett, Ted. *Great Hollywood Movies.* New York: Harry N. Abrams, 1983.

———. *Hollywood Musicals.* New York: Harry N. Abrams, 1981.

Sinclair, Andrew. *John Ford.* New York: Dial Press, 1979.

Skal, David J. *Hollywood Gothic: The Tangled Web of Dracula from Novel to Stage to Screen.* New York: Norton, 1990.

Spoto, Donald. *The Dark Side of Genius: The Life of Alfred Hitchcock.* London: Collins, 1983.

Telotte, J. P. *Dreams of Darkness: Fantasy and the Films of Val Lewton.* Urbana: University of Illinois Press, 1985.

INDEX

PHOTOGRAPH CREDITS

FILM CREDITS